Plans to Prosper: Strategies, Systems, and Tools for Small Business Marketing Success

By: Victoria Cook and Stan Washington

Linda

God has a

great plan for you!

Follow the lead!

Blessings,

Victoria

6/17/15

Plans to Prosper: Strategies, Systems, and Tools for Small Business Success

Scripture quotation identified NIV is from Holy Bible, New International Version®, NIV® Copyright © 1973, 1978, 1984, 2011 by Biblica, Inc.® Used by permission. All rights reserved worldwide.

Printed in the United States of America

First Printing, 2010

ISBN: 978-0-9909831-0-1

Table of Contents

Acknowledgments 6

Introduction 7

High-Achieving Marketing Process™ 10

First 30 Days—Readiness Phase 12

Gather

Market Survey..15

Know Your Market 20

Prepare

Setting the Course 24

Marketing Plan 27

Create

Branding 35

Creating Your Marketing Calendar 39

Initiate

Got Marketing Guilt? 44

Where Does the Time Go? 49

When to Outsource..55

First 30 Days Implementation Checklist 58

Second 30 Days—Execution Phase 60

Meet

Marketing While Networking 64

Open for Business 70

Content Marketing 74

Remind

Press Releases **79**

The Consultation as a Marketing Tool **85**

Packaged Deals **91**

Cement

Keeping in Touch **96**

Email Marketing Campaigns **99**

Increase

Social Media Business Pages **105**

Advertising **110**

Second 30 Days Implementation Checklist................**115**

Third 30 Days—Follow-Up Phase **117**

Retain

Following Up to Retain Growth.................................**121**

Loyalty and Referral Programs **124**

Assess

Dealing with Marketing Setbacks **131**

Tracking and Metrics..**135**

Modify

Modify Your Marketing Approach **140**

Close

Close This Wave of Marketing **143**

Third 30 Days Implementation Checklist................**145**

About the Authors **147**

Dedication

This book is dedicated with respect and admiration to small business owners everywhere who have the courage to share their product, service, or experience to a world that truly needs it.

Acknowledgments

We first wish to acknowledge and thank God and our families for the support, direction, and love given us, without which we would never have been able to pursue our businesses and help so many others.

I am humbled by the abundant support and encouragement I have had in business ownership and in writing this book. Brian Cook, you have always believed in me when I wasn't sure I did. Veronika Noize showed me the true meaning of relationship marketing and mentorship. You saw the marketer in me and reflected it back. Stan Washington started me on this adventure and made it such a pleasurable learning experience. Thank you for nudging me in the direction of becoming an author. Thanks Dad for helping me see I can do anything I set my mind to. Elene Cafasso, you lit the entrepreneurial flame in me. To my MasterMind colleagues, iron sharpens iron. Linda Washington, our book mentor and editor, thank you for pulling more from us and helping us bring more life to the pages.

My gratitude to the many clients with whom I have had the pleasure to work with and from whom I continue to learn and grow.

Victoria Cook

Blessed and *honored* are the words that come to mind when it comes to the support I have received. My wife, Gia; daughter, Jasmine; and son, Samuel, have truly hung in there through the thick of things. Thank you. Thanks to all of my special friends who are too numerous to name, who believed in me, encouraged me, and prayed for me. Thank you, Victoria Cook, for your great ideas, tenacity, and passion for people. You have stretched me and challenged me to grow. A special thank you to my sister, Linda, who brought our book to life. Thank you to all of my clients, customers, and participants for allowing me to serve you all of these years, thus enabling mutual growth.

Stan Washington

Introduction

When we started our businesses, we knew something was missing. As we saw successful people make it because of their business prowess, we probed further. After discovering that marketing was one of the foundational parts to their business, we wanted to learn more. But we focused on our functions and missed on our marketing. Perhaps this sounds familiar to you. We started our businesses because we were good at what we did, but soon we realized we needed some guidance with marketing.

Having a marketing strategy and a step-by-step plan for business is crucial to long-term success. However, many small and micro business owners skip this important foundational piece and jump directly into sales and serving their clients. Little thought is given to who they specifically serve, where to find them, or what kind of message will draw their market to their product or service.

With 18 years of business experience between us, we have gone through the ups and downs of running a business. Though we've made plenty of mistakes over the years, we've found strategies that have worked for us and our clients. This book is a compilation of those experiences and is meant to help the beginning entrepreneur or seasoned business owner walk through a 90-day process for greater marketing success.

Because of our work on the board of the International Coach Federation's Chicago Chapter Marketing team, we decided to collaborate and share our strategies to assist business owners with their marketing. The process of collaborating on this book has been a growing experience for each of us as we learned from each other. This is the book we wish we had when first starting our businesses. We have accumulated years of questions many issues business owners ask about marketing. For example:

- "Should I use social media?"

- "Should I advertise? How much should I spend?

- "How do I market if I don't have much money?"

The book is divided into three 30-day sections with a checklist to track your journey. You may wish to start at the beginning of the book and follow the step-by-step process or leverage individual sections as an on-demand go-to resource.

You Need This Book If . . .

- You are small business owners selling a service or product.

- You need fresh marketing ideas and are working with a small budget.

- You are looking for a systematic step-by-step approach to creating and implementing your marketing plan.

Features of This Book

Along with strategies you can use, at the end of each chapter, you'll find one or more of the following bulleted lists:

 NEXT STEPS

This section provides —three to five tips to implement after you've considered the advice in each chapter. For example: "Decide when you need to hire a marketing agency" (See the Outsourcing chapter). Choose the items that are right for you.

 WARNINGS

In this section, you'll find a list of problems and pitfalls to avoid when executing the items you choose. Each section has specific warnings we collected from our experiences and from other experts to keep you from wasting time and money.

High-Achieving Marketing Process™

Last but not least is our process. We have developed a systematic process business owners can follow to create, execute and follow-up on their overall marketing approach. We will guide you on each step as you develop and modify your plan. As you use this process, we hope you'll feel confident enough to take your business to the next level.

High-Achieving Marketing Process™

First 30 Days - Readiness Phase

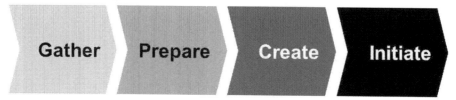

Second 30 Days - Execution Phase

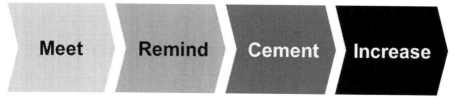

Third 30 Days - Follow-Up Phase

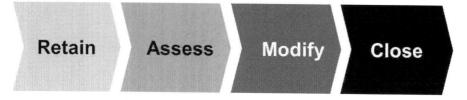

High Achieving Marketing Process™

After Internet searches that yielded only tiny slivers of information on marketing tactics, we were frustrated. Sound familiar? Over the years we tried many marketing strategies and tactics. Some worked well while others did not have the desired effect we needed.

We sat down and compiled the high performers. We drew from thousands of scenarios and created a list of the best and easiest strategies, systems, and tools.

A well-executed marketing strategy is key to your success. The High-Achieving Marketing Process™ (aka the process) provides strategies, systems, and tools for preparing, executing, and following up on your marketing plan.

We believe there is a plan to prosper you and your business. You can feel comforted in this journey, because you will always know where you are in the process. Don't worry—the process is iterative, meaning you may need to repeat steps of the process until you arc rcady to take on new challenges.

The process is broken into three major phases:

- The Readiness Phase lists techniques to gather, prepare, create, and initiate your marketing plan in a way that is easy yet meaningful. We know many business owners wear multiple hats, so we spread the effort over the first thirty days.

- The Execution Phase is focused on contact and reach to prospects, clients and customers. This is crucial to solidifying your brand as the expert while growing and building key relationships where your message can be heard. This is performed in the second thirty days. The Follow-Up Phase lists techniques to follow up with your target audience, as well as review your marketing efforts for better results.

We believe your marketing plan is a living document that you update continually as you grow your business.

By following this process through to completion you will know how to confidently increase awareness, visibility, and loyalty. This strengthens your brand and positions you as the expert.

First 30 Days—Readiness Phase

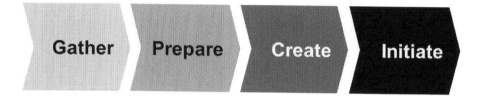

understand competition

survey

marketing plan

make a
new plan

know your customer

research

prepare

get ready

get set

Gather

After completing this step of the readiness phase, you will have a detailed understanding of your market and their needs. This will ensure that you have chosen a viable customer base and understand where to find them. It also ensures that your marketing aligns your solution to their problems.

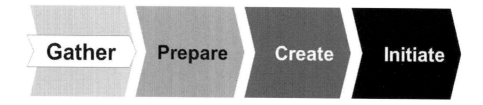

Market Survey

A few people called me for help with writing their resume, so I (Stan) helped them at no cost. Soon after, they referred people to me. So I did theirs for free also. Soon I found myself in demand, so I transformed this skill into a business. I acquired a business name, registered it with the state, and developed a catchy website. I was open for business.

There was only one problem: I didn't know the market! I had no idea what I should charge or how competitive the market was. One customer called me and asked, "What do you do that's different from Brand X?" I couldn't answer the question.

To help you avoid this same problem you will need to survey your market. We have listed a variety of types of surveys and information gathering techniques in this chapter. This is not an exhaustive list, but we feel it is a very strong beginning.

Understand the Competition

When I opened a technology business, I decided to look and leap at the same time. While I had not yet conducted market research, I started the business. This move enabled me to gain experience and learn what my customers desired while checking out the competition and reshaping the product to meet customers' needs. This approach yielded invaluable results.

Likewise, it is important that you understand what your competitors are doing and what they are saying about their product. I learned that my competition not only listed the benefits of their product but also listed other issues they resolved that I didn't know *were* issues. This made me adjust my approach to differentiate my company. I listed *executive resumes* on my website while my competitors listed an *executive portfolio* including a resume showcasing leadership style, board responsibilities, and span of control. They also discussed how they assist those who have been out of work for a while. I had to make a change.

Surveys

Are you ready for a game changer? Here are some surveys you may wish to conduct:

Competitor Pricing. Review your primary competition within a given trade area (usually a one-mile radius of your business if brick and mortar. Online businesses should check competitors who deal directly with the associations or groups within a specific field. Choose whether to be higher or lower and add your pricing strategy to your marketing plan.

Traffic Analysis. If your business is a brick and mortar business, how are you getting the attention of those who drive past your building daily? Is your location the right location? Here is a way to assess: create a document to record your information in military time to avoid confusion. Don't forget to count cars from both rush hours (6:30—9:30 a.m. and 4:30—7:30 p.m. aka 16:30—19:30). Record counts in 15-minute increments using tick marks. Repeat the study for the opposite direction.

Online Analysis. This one is a bit harder as some numbers can be deceiving. Though a high number of people may be associated with a group, this doesn't mean they are purchasing anything associated with the group. Use a CRM (customer relationship management) tool to analyze your connections with your audience. (See the Follow Up to Retain Growth section for more information.) Assess discussion and online business groups for effectiveness.

Purchasing Habits. Survey your audience to see if they like your product or service. I can't say enough about this! The size of your target group is not an indicator that they have money to purchase your product. Look for consumers or businesses who can afford your product or service and who value the outcome, results, or benefits of the product or service you provide.

Customer Locations. Do your customers meet regularly? If so, where? Do they choose products through social media or are they just hanging out via social media? I'm not talking about stalking. You're simply trying to find out where your customers spend most of their time.

Customer Profile. Do you actually know your customer? What business challenges are you resolving with your product or service? Get demographics to segment your marketing better. Consider age, gender, occupation, etc. in order to craft targeted messages.

Market Research. Local market research companies are well worth the price! They can help you avoid a significant amount of modification. Also, leverage your local library's business center for market analysis information. Government sites SBA.gov and DOL.gov can provide statistics to aid you in your market research. Some community colleges have small business development centers that you can use for no charge.

Secret Shopper. Look for local companies who provide the service of acting like a customer but will provide vital feedback to improve your processes and customer experience.

Understand Your Capacity

Quick service restaurant owners and business owners with a store front need to understand the high arrival rate of customers, which enables them to review when to add more staffing. Here are questions to help assess your capacity:

- How much is too much?
- What will enable you to have outstanding business?
- How many hours can you teach or how much product can you make that will be sold that day?

Understand Change

When cars were invented, horse and buggy businesses were still booming. Check the shift in your industry. Are you at the front of the market or at the tail end? Has technology altered the path? Will the market continue to go in the same direction? Realize of course you may be a trailblazer, so the "thing" you dream of may not exist yet.

Understand Viability

Is your product a real solution to your customers' problem? Is it safe? Superior? Is it as easy to use as you think? Though we thought using our product was easy, we had to do a significant amount of reworking because of consumer feedback.

 WARNING

- Steer away from getting confirmation from friends and family. Yes proud parents or the cousin who likes you will say you have a great product, but what does *the market* really say about your product or service?

- Be thorough in highly regulated industries. Check all guidelines and regulations before you market. Does your toy have small parts that can be swallowed by small children? Is your camp wheelchair accessible?

- Be careful of rigid processes and product lines. Be flexible! Once you learn more about what your consumers demand, identify a method to expand or alter your offerings to meet their needs.

NEXT STEPS

- Survey your market or car traffic.

- Build a spreadsheet listing your competitors and adding factors that are most important to you.

- Widen your market search to understand competitors who directly and indirectly compete.

- Review your product mix to include new offerings and expand your services.

Know Your Market

You are passionate about what you do. You have likely taken the time to hone your skills and abilities to provide the product or service you offer through your business. But do you have a clear picture of who those products and services are for specifically? Many business owners starting their business assume everyone will want what they are offering. That's a rookie mistake! Even if they want what you are offering, prospects won't buy from you for a number of reasons, including:

- A lack of understanding about your company or product.

- Their decision to purchase from your competitor.

- A delay in their purchasing decision.

- Their choosing to buy something altogether different, hoping they will get the result they desire.

Target Your Market

Are you attempting to sell sump pumps to apartment dwellers or homeowners? There is good news. You can find a group of buyers who want what you offer. The key is to clearly identify the type of client you seek or for whom your company's services are ideal. When your message is clear, your target market will self-identify. Referral partners and others in your network will know the best clients to refer your way. Also, by narrowing the focus, you position yourself as an expert in your field.

Identify who likes your product or service by doing surveys, studying your competitors, or by giving samples. Collect the information by location, gender, age, income, or other demographics that pertain to your product or service. Broaden your survey to capture responses from people you think would purchase from you and those who may not. What follows are tips for identifying your ideal client.

Know the Group

Do you help baby boomers, mothers of multiples, veterans, balding men or women with chronic pain? Is your product perfect for families with preschoolers, teenagers with acne, female business owners or male golfers? Being specific about the market for which your product or services is ideal can attract their attention.

Discern Their Reasons for Buying

Dig into your potential market segment's motivations for making their purchases. What problem, if any, keeps them up at night? Is there a season or life transition that drives their need for your product or service? Perhaps your markets are "Early Adopters"— attracted to the highest quality or the lowest prices. Are they looking for status? Knowing what motivates them can help you authentically connect with that market. It will also position your product or service as the right solution for a potential customer's problem, and help confirm that you are the right resource.

Get to Know Your Market's Needs

Once your ideal market segment is identified and you understand their motives, take time to get to know them more. What are their buying habits, hopes, and desires? Are there any unmet needs or are they being underserved in any areas in which your business can help?

Track Your Ideal Client

Finally, identify places (physical locations or online) where your ideal client can be found. Where do they gather? What social media platforms do they utilize? What do they read? Before working with me (Victoria), one of my clients spent a significant amount of time and effort building up a Facebook presence and Twitter following, thinking this would benefit her business and uncover prospects she could convert to clients. My client built relationships with partners, vendors, and mentors on both platforms and established her expert status. However, she didn't find many prospects, because she later discovered her ideal clients utilized LinkedIn.

If you are struggling to identify your ideal client at the start of your business, consider asking potential clients to talk with you about their challenges and needs. Don't turn this conversation into a sales pitch; this is simply an informational interview. Pay close attention to the feelings they share and the words they use to describe their pain, problem, or the solution they seek.

Look at your top five to ten best clients and see what they have in common. Consider asking them what challenges they faced prior to working with you or purchasing your product. How did it help? Listen for the words and feelings expressed. These can be very helpful as you formulate your marketing message. You may even get a couple new testimonials out of your conversations.

 NEXT STEPS

- Identify your ideal market segment.

- Identify the top 10 locations from which your segments get information.

- Determine the top five challenges your market faces so you can create products/services to solve those problems.

- Develop your message from the top problems. Use action verbs and the words used by your ideal clients to describe your product or service and how it will resolve these issues.

- Modify your product based on feedback from those who do not like your product.

Prepare

After completing this step, you will have a clear vision and plan that provides focus and easy implementation for a higher success rate.

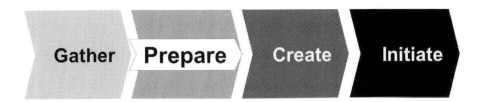

Setting the Course

All too often when talking with business owners who are unhappy with their results, we find they haven't set many goals nor created a specific marketing plan for reaching their goals or audience. One business owner shared that she really doesn't set annual goals. Instead she does as much work as she can to "hopefully" achieve the same level of success, or more, each year. Does this business owner's experience sound painfully familiar? If so, we're going to help you set and evaluate your business goals. For starters . . .

Get SMARTER

Many years ago U.S. educator and writer, Laurence J. Peter (1919–1988) made a simple and profound statement in *Peter's Quotations: Ideas for Our Time* that is still true today: "If you don't know where you are going, you will probably end up somewhere else!" Ending up where you really want to be, or darned close to it, requires a little bit of goal setting and planning. Once you have a vision for where you desire to take your business, the next step is setting SMARTER marketing goals that will get you there. Make sure your goal can pass the SMARTER test. Is your goal:

Specific? Is your marketing goal clearly articulated?

Measurable? Can the results of your marketing efforts be quantified?

Achievable? Does your marketing goal cause you to stretch, grow and get out of your comfort zone but also have a degree of attainability?

Rewarding? Will achieving this marketing goal be valuable to you? How so?

Time-Based? Do you have a date for when you will complete the marketing tactics or campaign in order to achieve this goal?

Evaluated? Have you schedule intervals to review and measure the results of your marketing efforts and gauge their effectiveness?

Revised? Have you implemented monthly, quarterly, and annual updates to the strategies, tactics and plans for your business marketing?

Magnetizing Your Goals

Setting goals that align with your personal values make your goals more magnetic. Everyone values different things in life: family, creativity, honesty, spirituality, making a difference, having fun, wealth, etc. Goals that are not aligned with your values are goals doomed to failure.

Incorporate your values into your goals. How might this look? Here is an example:

The vision—Your Best Health, Inc. is recognized and respected as a leading provider of family healthcare solutions.

Some key company values—Making a difference; knowledge sharing; health and wellness

Business needs—Improve sales through increasing current customer base

Value-based goal—"We will increase sales by $10,000 by helping 50 new clients improve their heart health through the use of our product this year."

Instead of focusing on increasing sales, this goal puts the emphasis on helping improve the health of 50 new clients. By educating their clients about their product, this company honors their core values of knowledge sharing and health and wellness. The outcome will be the same, but how much they are drawn towards achieving the goal will be dramatically different. The business owner passionate about helping others will see this as an opportunity to reach out and make a difference instead of hustling to make a buck.

Through the attainment of the values-based goal, they will feel fulfilled and good about having made a positive difference in the lives of those 50 families. Also, sales will automatically go up—a win-win outcome!

WARNING

- Vague goals will net you vague results. Be specific and realistic in your goal setting and timeframe.

NEXT STEPS

- Create your SMARTER goals.

- Incorporate your values into the goals.

- Schedule intervals in your calendar for regular assessments, then review and revise your plan.

- Place your goals in your marketing plan.

Marketing Plan

The aim of marketing is to know and understand the customer so well the product or service fits him and sells itself.—Peter F. Drucker, founder of the country's first executive MBA program at Claremont Graduate University, quoted at Forbes.com

Stan was excited about the start of his executive resume business and decided to advertise on the radio in the Chicagoland area. He asked himself, "How can I reach a large group of people fast?" He met with the radio station and they developed a wonderful commercial for his company. As he listened to it on the radio, he expected the phone to ring each time it played. He was excited when calls came in, but to his dismay, they were not from his target audience.

Since he couldn't afford advertising on the news station his target audience listened to, he settled for the local "oldies" station—the kind of station to which he enjoyed listening. His marketing budget had now been spent on an audience that would not purchase from him. Now what was he going to do? He still needed to generate awareness to build his business.

Every business should have a strong business plan that includes a well-thought-out marketing plan focused on relationship building. The Small Business Administration, Small Business Development Center, the IRS, or the *Harvard Business Review* will tell you that having a specific marketing plan is crucial for small business success and profitability. According to "Small Business Survival: A Joint Report to the Governor in 2007," many businesses fail due to deficiencies in planning and inadequate marketing. They either don't do *enough* marketing or don't do the *right mix* of marketing. In this chapter we'll discuss various strategies you can tailor to fit your business.

Marketing Plan Overview

Do you have a detailed marketing plan? Many, but not all, business owners have a business plan, which includes a marketing plan section. This may contain valuable information about the market segment, competition, marketing channels, industry, and marketing strategies. Yet the plan often lacks detailed information business owners can use to get started marketing their business. The following information should be included in your marketing plan.

GOT GOALS?

Write your company name, financial goals, the mission of your business, and the specific market segment, messaging, strategies, and tactics you will use in order to reach your financial goals. Your goals should be written down. While they don't have to be set in stone, they should be placed in a document you can refer to and update often.

OTHER PARTS OF THE MARKETING PLAN

In addition to the previously mentioned mission and goals, a solid plan should include the following information:

Market Survey. This section provides a full understanding of the competition and your customers in order to define or refine your service or product offering. Do your customers relate to what you offer? See more details in the Market Survey section.

Ideal Market. This section defines the ideal clients who will most benefit from what you offer and who are willing to pay for it. Don't be afraid to be specific. Is your market family-owned businesses, C-Level executive women, men over 40 who ride Harleys, or mothers with multiple children?

Top Five Challenges of Your Market. This will help you understand your customers' needs and desires and allow you to position your product or service as the solution to the challenges they face. For example, one of the challenges the ideal client of a dog walking business faces is how to best meet the needs of his or her pet while the client works long hours.

Service/Products Offered. Ideally this should be a suite of products or services working together to solve your customers' core problem(s). A business owner offering graphic design services might offer design packages for logos and letterhead development, business branding services, and the creation of direct mail pieces and newsletters.

Core Message. Consider the top three messages that will resonate most with your ideal market segment or client and the problem you can solve. When Apple started promoting the early generation iPod, their core message was "One thousand songs in your pocket."

Killer Elevator Speech.** A seven- to thirteen-word statement that distills the essence of what you do, for whom, and the benefit they will receive from your work or the results they will gain from your product. For example here is my elevator speech, "I help women business owners attract great clients that pay, stay, and refer."

Tagline. A tagline is different from the killer elevator speech in that it is more of a positioning statement or a promise of how customers will experience or feel about the product or service. A tagline is generally very short, as in Nike's "Just do it!"

Your Unique Process.** The unique way in which you work with clients and help them achieve their success. Being able to articulate this will provide your prospects and clients with greater trust in what you offer. It will also demonstrate your expertise and increase your credibility. In short, it shows your market that you have a clear path to accomplish what they desire.

Pricing Strategy. How will you price your services or product? This can include introductory programs and packages that help your

---

* Information from *How to Create a Killer Elevator Speech.* by Veronika Noize. Copyright © 2002. Used by permission of the author. All rights reserved by the original author.

market to solve their problem(s). How will you convert prospects to clients? For example, a business offering web development services might include a low-cost introductory website assessment. This will facilitate a deeper understanding of the prospects' current and future needs.

The business owner can then recommend one of three packages: (1) A mobile-ready starter package with five basic pages; (2) a business package that includes options in the starter package plus ten additional web pages, a blog, search engine optimization, and photo gallery; and (3) a premium package that includes everything in the first two packages, plus embedded video and up to 25 pages with training on how to manage the site. The middle package will be priced attractively to entice purchasers.

Risk Reversal.** What can you do to eliminate the financial risk for your market and help them say yes to buying from you? Examples include a guarantee, sample, an easy cancellation policy, or product replacement.

Why Choose You? This is often called your *unique sales proposition* or *unique sales positioning,* but it comes down to why your market should choose you over the competition. Do you have specific knowledge, a unique understanding of that market, or specialized training? Ensure that your positioning aligns with what your market is looking for from the product or service you provide.

Connection Points.((* Where can you find your market congregating at physical locations and online? Where do they already look for the solution to their problem(s)? Do they belong to a particular association where they regularly meet in person? Are they connecting in LinkedIn groups to look for resources and share information? Do they read a particular trade magazine? Find out where they live and congregate so you and your business can be present there as well.

** Information from *Marketing Blueprint Workshop* by Veronika Noize. Copyright © 2002. Used by permission of the author. All rights reserved by the original author.

Marketing Channels. What are the top three to five marketing channels that will best reach your market? If you offer interior decorating services, your market might be big on Pinterest, Etsy, and Instagram.

Content Strategy. What kind of useful content can you offer your market that will be beneficial to them, position you as an expert, and attract them to your business? Providing valuable content that introduces prospects to your products and services without giving away all that you do is a great way to attract warm leads. The content can then be delivered on a variety of marketing channels, thus leveraging your time and message, and driving traffic back to your website or brick and mortar storefront.

Marketing Strategies. The specific marketing strategies you will use to attract, acquire, and retain your ideal market. Strategy examples include advertising, direct mail, public relations, search engine optimization and signage.

Marketing Tactics. What are the specific methods you will use to promote your goods or services? If you are using direct mail as a marketing strategy, your tactics could be postcards, a letter campaign, or mailed invitations.

Marketing Budget. This should be about 10% to 12% of gross annual sales or initial investment.

Tools. What are the tools you will use in your business? For example, business cards, website, videos, seminars, podcasts, scripts, postcards, or other marketing collateral.

Tracking. What key metrics will you track in order to determine the ROI of your marketing and the time invested in the specific strategies and tactics? Be sure to give a strategy a solid 90 days of implementation before deciding it is not working. By measuring your results you may find the strategy is a good one, but messaging, delivery, or implementation might need some tweaking.

Marketing Calendar. A specific plan of what you will do each day, week, month, quarter, and year that implements your tactics and strategies and achieves your business goals. See a sample and more details in the Creating Your Marketing Calendar section.

Many of the clients with whom I work have shared their need for a marketing plan. Some knew the kind of information a marketing plan contained, but never made the time to put one together. After one client worked with me to create and implement her plan, she shared that she had greater confidence in her ability to talk about her business. More importantly she nearly *tripled* her income. Don't skip this important step!

 WARNING

- It's tempting for business owners to start their business, open the doors, and jump into business ownership. But if they don't do the upfront planning, a lot of time and money will be wasted trying to market products the market doesn't want or need in a way that repels rather than attracts. This can leave a business owner feeling like a failure when in fact the only thing he or she failed to do was plan.

- Do not be afraid of committing to a budget for marketing. Many people focus all their attention on building new products, services, and ideas and forget to tell people about the benefits.

- Understand the marketing strategies before you begin.

NEXT STEPS

- Conduct your market survey.

- Create or refine your marketing plan document.

- Fill in answers to the above sections of the plan as you work through the different chapters of this book and conduct your own research.

- Create a marketing calendar for the next 6-12 months.

- Hire a marketing agency.

- Refine your marketing plan throughout the entire High-Achieving Marketing Process™.

Create

After completing this step, you will have a clear vision of how your market perceives your brand. You will also have actions to add to your calendar to drive your plan.

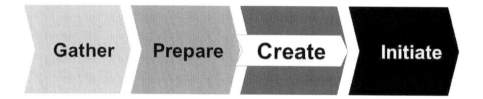

Branding

For obvious reasons, Little Poopers Accounting may not be the best name if you are an accounting firm. Choosing the right name for your company, product, or service is vital because you want your clientele to find you. Once found, you want them to feel confident about your product or service. Brand recognition is more than a clever name.

Keep It Simple

The cleverer the name the more likely people will miss the meaning unless you have tons of cash or a huge following that already knows the meaning of your clever name. Branding takes years, so start simple and understand you might change your name two or three times. Ask yourself:

Does the name have meaning or is it catchy and memorable? Zippo is a catchy brand that expresses ease and quickness of use. What feeling or message do you want your customers to remember about your company?

Is the name short enough? Short names are easier to type for those who are looking for you. Long names tend to be fraught with typo problems. Lego is an extremely recognized brand while Meandmyfriendscutdowntreescheap.com may be explanatory, but will be hard to remember and hard to type correctly twice.

Is it available? Pull up a web domain company and check to see if the URL is available. If so, snag it immediately.

How do you wish to be recognized? Choose a naming style for which your company will be recognized. Think descriptive—one that will evoke an emotional response or one that seems whimsical. Let's look at the travel industry for a moment. Hotels.com describes what they do and where they have their business. Priceline.com evokes an emotional response to price. Kayak.com is a whimsical name. Make it easy to spell and be careful of sound alike letters like *X* and *S*. My (Stan) first company used *F-I-X* in a brand name and many people on the phone heard *F-I-S*.

Should you use an acronym? You choose. Do you want to be known as the Planning Insight Group or PIG? Whichever way you choose, be consistent.

Logo or No Logo?

Take this often overlooked item seriously. Hire a pro or pick a free logo that matches your values, vision, and mission. Facebook and Twitter have moved to a square format for logos while LinkedIn allows a rectangle. Have both and make sure you develop one that can scale to a large banner size (.tiff), one to adapt to colors (.png) and one that is opaque (.jpg).

Banner Up

Build a banner that represents your primary business. You can mix words and pictures here. In fact, a professional can add wonderful pictures representing your product, service, or audience. Remember, the customer has to see themselves purchasing your product or service. Show smiles if you use pictures of people. Watch those colors! Make them tasteful.

Tagline

A tagline is a catchphrase or slogan expressing the meaning of your business, product or service. Be careful not to make this too long. In fact, keep it simple. Nike's "Just Do It" tagline has to be the easiest set of words that personifies getting over procrastination and doing whatever "it" is. Keep it short. Taglines should evolve with your company. They should not be more than 10 words for maximum effectiveness. Taglines are very hard to create, so relax and keep at it until the tagline resonates.

Extended Elevator Pitch

Your elevator pitch is different than your tagline and elevator speech. This is a 30 second brief 40 word or less statement enables you to explain who you serve, what you do and why you do what you do and the positioning in the market. Again, keep this simple. For Example: When asked, "What does your company provide?" my (Stan) reply would be, "We offer affordable cloud database applications that automates sales, marketing and finance for home based, women, veteran, start-up and micro businesses. What makes us different is we've simplified four database technologies into one secure easy to use tool combining CRM, invoicing, client management and email marketing."

 **WARNING**

- Be careful not to choose a branded name. You might run into legal trouble. Even names with pronunciations similar to other names can be problematic. For example: McDonald's Corporation will not allow McDonald Corporation for your name even though the name is spelled slightly different.

- Avoid noisy logos. Pictures of mascots, curves, and curlicues tend to detract from the brand name, rather than enhance it. If these elements are done poorly, potential clients will be dismissive even if you have the coolest name. Keep logos simple.

- Protect yourself. Once you have chosen a brand, file it with the U.S. Patent and Trademark Office (USPTO).

NEXT STEPS

- Write your values, short mission, or elevator pitch for your business in 40 words or less.

- Identify keywords that represent your brand.

- Leverage these keywords to brand or rebrand your business.

- Search the internet for your potential name to see if it is available.

- Trademark your name to protect your brand.

Creating Your Marketing Calendar

Having a plan and knowing how you will specifically market and grow your business is only three-quarters of the equation. The last quarter for success is *consistently doing* the work! This means knowing exactly what to do each day, week, month, quarter, and year. This is where a marketing calendar comes in handy. It will help align the actions with specific strategies and goals so you know what to do and, just as importantly, what *not* to do.

Putting together a marketing calendar for promoting your content and services or product takes an enormous amount of stress off your shoulders by helping you plan what you will do while providing a purpose for each action. Having a plan for your marketing reduces time waste by leveraging your efforts and getting the biggest bang for your time.

Leveraging your marketing efforts means identifying cross promotional opportunities to deliver the same message in a variety of ways (visual, auditory, or print) through multiple channels. This can increase the probability of your market seeing your marketing while presenting a consistent message. Your marketing messages are competing for attention against the thousands of other messages your market sees every day in email, direct mail, radio, Facebook, and television. Ensure you have a consistent message running through all of your marketing strategies (lead generation, client acquisition, retention, and referral strategies).

Your marketing calendar also needs to identify when the marketing strategies and tactics will be implemented each day, week, month, quarter, and/or year. Having a schedule and due dates will help you maintain motivation and momentum as you consistently marketing your business. Create for yourself an easy way of tracking the tasks and the results of your efforts. Here are some examples of what could be included in a marketing calendar:

Daily

- Review marketing plan and calendar.

- Make five calls to keep in touch with prospects, power partners, and clients.

- Take ten minutes of creative focus to capture new ideas or future projects.

- Post on social media.

- Respond to blog or social media posts and comments.

Weekly

- Update website by adding upcoming events, blog posts, or short articles.

- Schedule in advance articles, future events, and promotions to share with your market on social media sites.

- Meet with one or two people you want to get to know better or with strategic partners to further working relationships.

- Join the conversation through guest posts in forums and blogs related to your industry.

Monthly

- Send an email newsletter or a direct mail newsletter to your list with valuable content and information about your product or service.

- Plan a lead-generating event live or online to share your expertise and attract prospects.

- Attend an organizational or networking meeting.

- Track marketing efforts and analyze monthly results.

- Create some expert content in a podcast, video, or other content marketing solution that fits your business.

Quarterly

- Set up an in-person event for clients and prospects.

- Review marketing efforts and analyze results over time.

- Determine marketing strategies and tactics for the next quarter.

- Advertise where your audience lives.

- Send a press release about newsworthy items regarding your company.

Yearly

- Attend one major fundraiser or conference related to your industry.

- Update profiles on social media.

- Analyze marketing results.

- Update your marketing plan and calendar.

- Create a yearly events calendar for the coming year

- Decide on new content, eBook, white paper, e-course, or case study you can offer your market in the coming year.

NEXT STEP

- Schedule time in your calendar to take the specific actions you have outlined in your marketing calendar and keep them like appointments with your very best clients.

Initiate

After completing this step, you will move past excuses that have led to marketing avoidance in the past. You will be pumped to proceed while ensuring you have the time to get everything done.

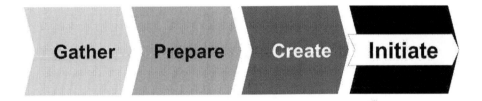

Got Marketing Guilt?

A few years ago, during an interview for an article about her coaching business, a reporter asked me (Victoria) if I thought guilt was an emotion. At first I almost instinctively said yes, but as I thought about the work I had done with clients, and how guilt occasionally crept into my own life, I realized that guilt is really a conditioned response.

Guilt is something we've become accustomed to allow in our lives. It's not the same as our conscience, which is an innate urging to do right rather than wrong. Our conscience often guides our behavior to what we sense is right.

Merriam-Webster.com defines *guilt* as "feelings of culpability especially for **imagined offenses** or from **a sense of inadequacy**." (Emphasis added.) That feeling of inadequacy in business and marketing can point to a lack of confidence in oneself or one's product or service.

The guilt many business owners feel as it relates to marketing includes guilt about

- The amount of time they are spending on their business and the time spent away from their family.

- Charging for their services. This leads to their failure to earn what they desire or an inability to contribute to their family finances in the way they want.

- What they believe they need to do to market their business in order to succeed. For example, do they have to be pushy, shamelessly self-promoting, insincere, or boastful?

The Sources of Guilt

While guilt can arise from a variety of sources, I have identified the following three main sources of guilt for business owners:

The Should or Shouldn't Dilemma. This means comparing oneself to others or trying to conform to the standards of others. Business owners without a specific vision for their business or a clear marketing plan end up wasting time and money on marketing. They hear about or see the success of other business owners using a specific marketing channel or strategy and believe they "should" do the same thing. Yet this strategy may not be the right choice for their business or their market. This creates resentment, stress, and frustration. Comparing oneself to other business owners and feeling like you should do what they are doing will only cause guilt, insecurity, and unhappiness.

The "Type A" Trap. This means unreasonably high self-imposed standards. Many of the clients with whom I (Victoria) work happen to be firstborn females. They are high achieving, well accomplished with a very high drive. Sometimes they forget they aren't Superwoman! Many entrepreneurs have similar characteristics and struggle with the desire to be perfect. Marketing is an iterative process. You may not get it right the first time. Develop the ability to fast-fail ideas through trial and error and quickly recover by learning what went wrong and how you can improve on the process. Marketing isn't about *avoiding* mistakes. It is learning *how to address them.*

The Three Big O's: Overwhelmed, Overworked, and Overcommitted. These feelings of guilt arise from a failure to utilize boundaries or an inability to say no when warranted. As you consider your ideal market, consider who is a good client, and also when to say no.

The inability to say no can result in a yes to low-quality materials, work outside your expertise, unreasonable deadlines, or taking on less than ideal clients for the sake of money. This can result in stress and life imbalance, and erodes self-confidence. Saying no is not a bad a thing nor does it mean you aren't a team player or have no concern for your clients. Sometimes caring means saying no, because it allows you to set reasonable expectations and say yes to what aligns with your business mission, marketing goals, and skills.

Dealing with Guilt

As human beings we can tolerate a lot. When the warning signs of guilt are continually ignored, two primary issues occur. First, resentment builds over a lack boundaries and saying yes to too many things (for example, unreasonable deadlines or less-than-ideal clients). This creates stress. As the resentment mounts, a person's fuse shortens, which can cause outbursts of anger at inappropriate times. Instead of dealing with conflicts right away, a pattern of avoidance develops, further straining relationships with colleagues, employees, or clients.

Second, unchecked guilt creates feelings of paralysis and frustration, which in turn leads to inaction. This more guilt for not making progress in your business or earning the desired profits.

As a busy entrepreneurs or business owner, are you

- Struggling to justify the amount of time you spend on your business that takes away from your family, community, spiritual, or volunteer time when your business isn't paying you what you are worth?

- So busy trying to keep up and react to everything going on in your business and serving your clients that you feel guilty taking time away for implementing strategies to grow your business?

- Struggling to talk about what you do and the results clients receive in a way that is comfortable for you and attracts new clients?

- Avoiding the pursuit of clients out of fear of being seen as pushy or only concerned with sales?

If you answered yes to any of the questions above, it is critical that you overcome the guilt in order to use your time effectively and achieve the success in your business you desire.

WARNING

- Watch out for the "shoulda, woulda and couldas." If you hear yourself or others saying *should, would,* or *could,* beware— there could be some underlying guilt involved.

 NEXT STEPS

- If you struggle with guilt in your business, identify its source: lack of a clear vision and plan; unreasonable expectations and standards; or a lack of confidence about what you offer and how you help your clients. Awareness is the first step to resolution.

- Reduce your feeling of inadequacy by setting clear business goals and creating a plan with specific strategies and tactics to achieve them. (Here is where your marketing plan comes in handy.)

- Remind yourself why providing your product or service to clients is important to you beyond the financial aspect). Reminding yourself about your plan and purpose will do a lot to quiet some of the negative self-talk.

- When speaking with a prospect about his or her challenge, make sure what you offer aligns with that challenge. Share facts about your business and the benefits they will receive then ask if they would like to receive those benefits. That's not pushy—that's good business!

- Understand that if you want to truly grow your business, it's going to take a paradigm shift. If you knew without a shadow of a doubt that the information shared in this book and your business marketing would in fact double your income in the next 12 months, would you feel guilty about taking the time to do them? Of course not! The results would support your business as well as your family. So commit to carving out the time needed to implement what you are reading for the next 90 days, then reassess.

Where Does the Time Go?

"I wish it need not have happened in my time," said Frodo.

"So do I," said Gandalf, "and so do all who live to see such times. But that is not for them to decide. **All we have to decide is what to do with the time that is given us.**"

—J. R. R. Tolkien, The Fellowship of the Ring (1955, p. 76; emphasis added)

It's like Gandalf, Tolkien's well-known wizard, suggests: we must decide what to do with the time given us. Managing one's time to run and market a business and market effectively is not a matter of strength of will, but choice, commitment, and habit. Many business owners are busy doing the work of providing their products or service, but have not taken time to tell people about their product. This causes the pipeline of new customers to diminish. The business owner then works harder, thus causing even less time for marketing.

Many of us know that the world is not in our control, but there *is* one thing we *can* control: our behavior. We choose what to do in our business, either by intention or by default. This is the key to time management. Before we get to how you can manage your time effectively, let's talk about some aspects that work against time management.

There is a concept from the world of psychology called *positive illusion*, which means we tend to think better of ourselves or of a process or situation than is merited by evidence. For example, most of us believe we are better than average drivers, but that is statistically impossible, because not all of us can be in the better than average category. Most of us also overestimate our level of intelligence and excuse our faults more easily than we would excuse the faults and infractions of others. This relates to time management in that due to a familiarity with a process, we sometimes underestimate the number of steps a particular task requires. Thus, we fail to allot the necessary amount of time and the critical steps needed to complete a task.

This positive illusion about how quickly we can accomplish tasks is very common. How often have you heard yourself tell a client or colleague that a task only takes a minute or five, when the truth the task requires about 20 minutes?

In addition to the handicap of positive illusion, we often believe that getting a lot done is simply a matter of intelligence, intention, or will. It is not. Just because we are smart or have good intentions does not mean we can bend the laws of time and space to complete our to-do list! So what is a business owner to do to effectively manage time?

Budgeting Business Time

First, you need to know where your time goes. How are you spending the time you have during the business day? Many business owners are very busy on tasks that don't generate revenue, align with their marketing efforts, or make an impact. That's why it's important to take a hard look at how you're spending your time.

Allocate time for the important components of running and marketing your business. A good rule of thumb is 40% of your time on product/service delivery, 35% on marketing, 15% on networking and offsite meetings, and 10% on administrative work.

Divide your marketing strategies into the specific tasks and individual tactics required for execution. When I (Victoria) began publishing a monthly e-zine, I would list *send e-zine* on my to-do list for the week. At the end of the week I still wasn't able to hit send. I felt frustrated and would beat myself up for failing to complete such a simple task that should only take a couple hours, right? I realized there were several steps that needed to be completed in order to send the e-zine.

- First, I had to write the article to share

- Second, I had to add and schedule it for publication on her blog.

- Third, the website events page often required updating with whatever upcoming events were being promoted in the e-zine

- Fourth, I had to create the e-zine email to send.

- Fifth, I needed to write a welcome message.

- Sixth, I had to add any new subscribers from speaking events to the list.

If any of the six steps leading to the completion of the e-zine were not done, the e-zine could not be sent and this item on my to-do list could not be checked off. I needed to allocate more time for completing the e-zine and schedule specific appointments on my calendar to complete each separate task.

Budget your time accordingly, block off space in your calendar for each component, and keep each item like an appointment with your best client. If working on a new task, add 30% more to your projected time needs, make sure to account for the learning curve. Place a high priority on marketing tasks. That will help keep prospects coming and maintain cash flow.

To maintain focus and momentum, stick to one task at a time. Multitasking really doesn't work. It's a good idea to set a timer for the amount of time budgeted for a specific task and work diligently during that time. When the timer rings, move on to the next item on your agenda.

Plan for the Unexpected

Some business owners find it beneficial to create an ideal schedule. When creating an ideal schedule, business owners believe it needs to be a detailed plan of what they will do each minute of each day. While working with a client who was frustrated with trying to execute his detailed ideal schedule, Victoria found there was no room for the inevitable unexpected. So if one unplanned activity or emergency popped up, the schedule was completely hosed.

Instead of planning 100% of your day, allocate just 60% of the work time to specific client, business, and marketing tasks. This will leave some "white space" and time for the unexpected but still allow you to concentrate on tackling what's most important. If you don't have good time management, you won't have the time for any of your marketing tasks.

Additional Tools for Time Management Success

Now that you have an understanding of where your time is going and how you will prioritize it, there is one more tool that can help you stay on track. One of the most important tools business owners can use to manage their schedule and ensure the time needed for marketing and client delivery tasks is a simple one: *core business hours*.

Many of the clients with whom I (Victoria) have worked come from a corporate background. They were high-achieving professionals who juggled multiple priorities, yet often were surprised that they were unable to do the same in their businesses. The tasks most often dropped when a business owner was pressed for time were those related to marketing. Having core business hours is a good solution.

One client struggling with her time management told me she felt as if she was always working yet didn't have time to market because she never had any time off. When asked about when she began her business day, my client mentioned that some days she started at 9:00 a.m., but the other morning she had some errands to run and didn't get started until after lunch. For the following week, she had plans for breakfast with a friend and would not begin her business day until 10:30 a.m. Whenever she started later in the day, she would make up for it by working later. She was also behind on completing some client work and billing, so she put in extra hours on the weekends. No wonder she felt like she was always working.

The solution was for her to select the main hours she would work each day. This was time spent on strategic and income generating tasks, working for clients, and managing the details of her marketing and business. She agreed she would not use those hours for getting together with friends, doing laundry, or running errands.

Within a matter of weeks, my client shared that she felt more on top of her business, had responded to client and prospect inquiries quickly, and had gained two new clients. By focusing my client on the High-Achieving Marketing Process™, she was able to put structure to her day for focused time on marketing, product or service delivery, and business administration.

WARNING

- Business ownership flexibility or control of schedule is possible, but we suggest that it be the exception and not the rule.

- Don't spend too much time on social media. Have a specific plan for how you will leverage the various marketing channels and stick to it.

 NEXT STEPS

- Track how you spend your business time for one week. This can be done simply with pencil and paper, or if you prefer a digital option, Paymo.biz is a free online tool that is easy to use for time tracking.

- Set core business hours and assign realistic time frames to your key business and marketing tasks.

- Schedule your business and marketing task appointments in your physical or electronic calendar. Be sure to include time for implementing important marketing tactics that support the strategies you are using to reach your goals.

When to Outsource

Sitting at the desk, absolutely exhausted I (Stan) fretted at the thought of continuing. *Being in business is tough,* I thought. I was not only the president and founder of the technology company, I was also the salesperson, accountant, and janitor. Many small business owners face the same situation. They take on too many tasks themselves.

Marketing is one of the tasks we tried and failed at miserably. It's not that we couldn't tell people about our product or that we didn't have passion. We needed help. It actually hurt our ego, since we had the marketing chair on three boards working with us and in the past we helped one of the best known brands with marketing and branding.

Making the Mental Switch

Our concern was wasting money. We had already spent a mint advertising on some very famous social media channels and saw some success, but we were not getting the pull we desired. Our day was extremely busy and focused on growing sales. We were actually busy helping others with marketing and left ours to die on the vine. We had to make a mental switch to outsource marketing.

We felt it necessary to remain hands on with our clientele, so we sought a marketing company that would work with us and leverage our years of corporate marketing and technology knowledge. This meant, however, that we would have to pay for an area in which we were well versed. In other words, we had to let go in order to grow!

What to Look For

You will not find a marketing company that does everything for a low price. If you do, then please send them our way. Instead, seek a company that will lay out a plan with which you can feel comfortable. Social media is nice, but is that where your audience really spends their time? Seek a company that works on more than one channel of marketing.

Marketing Avenues and Strategies to Ask About

- Connections to large groups

- Partnering

- Content marketing

- Webinars

- Public relations strategy

- Email blasts

- Advertising

- Social media

Discuss with your outsourcing company the frequency, cost, and wording to be used.

Stay Involved

To see how your plan is going, ask for reports on a monthly basis. Accept the plan and meet on a regular basis to make any necessary adjustments to it. Great marketing companies can track progress and you should see reports that help you calculate your return on investment (ROI).

 WARNING

- Beware of the single channel trap. Marketing makes people aware of your product or service. This means you should try to hit as many of the places where your clientele gets their information as possible.

- Watch out for overspending on a single marketing channel. Remember: your return on investment should eventually equate to increased awareness of your brand which in turn should add up to growth, loyalty, and an overall great customer experience.

- Free is never free. In my experience, the more you rely on free marketing channels, the less likely you will experience true growth. I have heard of the "one" person who makes free channels work for him or her very well. Yet such a strategy requires an enormous amount of time and effort most people don't have.

 NEXT STEPS

- Assess your marketing needs and see if outsourcing is right for you.

- Review your market survey to address areas of concern and to ensure you are using the right language.

- If you cannot afford outsourced marketing today, save up and plan for it as soon as possible.

First 30 Days
Implementation Checklist

Gather

☐ Read the introduction and the First 30 Days section to get an overview.

☐ Create a physical folder or digital folder for all notes and materials.

☐ Put time on your calendar each week to work through the process.

☐ Conduct initial market research.

☐ Identify your first ideal market segment.

☐ Find the top 10 locations from which your ideal market segment gains information.

☐ Draft the top five challenges the ideal market faces

☐ Begin a draft of your market survey.

☐ Create a spreadsheet of top competitors.

☐ Research competition and those with whom you directly and indirectly compete.

☐ Finalize and complete market survey.

☐ Draft a product mix or list of service offerings of interest to your ideal market.

Prepare

☐ Draft SMARTER goals.

☐ Review market research and survey results.

☐ Begin a draft marketing plan.

☐ Write out values, short mission statement, or elevator pitch for your business in 40 words or less.

Create

- ☐ Review and finalize the top five challenges your ideal market has for which you have resources.

- ☐ Refine product mix/service offering based on market research and survey results.

- ☐ Review marketing survey data and ensure the marketing messages address the core concerns of your market.

- ☐ Identify keywords that represent your brand.

- ☐ Decide on a logo or font treatment for your business.

- ☐ Finalize logo or font treatment.

- ☐ Identify two or three social media sites to connect with your audience.

- ☐ Draft a marketing calendar of what tasks to be done daily, weekly, and monthly.

Initiate

- ☐ Start time log to track time use.

- ☐ Set core business hours.

- ☐ Identify and eliminate marketing guilt.

- ☐ Identify what tasks can be outsourced now and in the future.

- ☐ List in a document why serving clients is important to you.

white paper

blog

podcast

go viral

you are
the expert

content marketing

video

they want to hear from you

webinar

share

Second 30 Days—Execution Phase

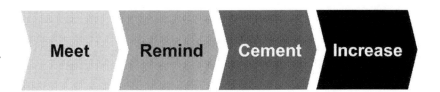

build pipeline   reach out

don't be shy

get out
and meet

join groups   **people**

make meaningful connections

participate   go

Meet

After this step, you will have engaged the audience and proven your expertise.

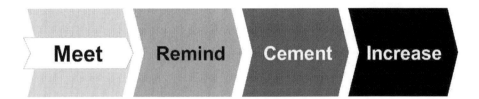

Marketing While Networking

There are countless books written on the subject of business networking. Allow us to prune that information for you. We can do that in one statement: Networking is all about creating and growing relationships. Period. When I (Victoria) meet business owners and entrepreneurs and they hear I am a marketing coach and teach a networking class, I often hear the same thing: "I do lots of networking, but it hasn't generated any business for me." "Networking is a waste of my time. Haven't made a sale yet." Unfortunately these folks have confused the process of sales with networking.

Networking Nightmare

At a networking event, Sylvia (not her real name) came up and introduced herself to me (Victoria) and another business owner whom I recently met. Sylvia worked for a well-known national company and proceeded to tell them about the services her company offered. Sylvia put me and the other business owner on the spot when she asked point blank if we did business with her company. It felt a bit uncomfortable, but I admitted to using some of the services offered, thinking that would be the end of a very awkward conversation. Boy was I wrong!

Sylvia then proceeded to ask why I didn't use *all* of the services they had and that it wouldn't hurt to get a complimentary quote from her. Sylvia was sure she could save me some money. I smiled politely and thanked her for the suggestion and was delighted when she pounced on the next woman who walked by.

Sylvia had made a big mistake. She was moving around the room, looking to make a sale. Like many business people, she's likely passionate about what she does. It's the *way* she did it that caused those she met to take a step back.

Marketing While Networking Can Be Easy

Don't confuse the process of networking with sales. The chance of meeting the perfect ideal client who is ready, willing, and able to buy from you at that exact moment is small. Here are some keys to make the most of your networking:

Build Relationships. Networking is a marketing strategy for gaining visibility, developing relationships, and attracting your ideal market. It is *not* the time for a sales conversation. Consistent contact through networking and 1:1 meetings creates familiarity, credibility, and trust. This is important, because the odds of meeting an ideal client for your business while networking can be very slim. However, each person you meet knows at least 200 people. Since relationships are transferable, you have a potential pool of relationships that is 200 times the number of people in your networking pool *if* you have built a good relationship with them. Sylvia wasn't looking to build a relationship. The people she met barely had the opportunity to introduce themselves before she turned turn the conversation back to her and her sales pitch.

Don't assume a need. Sylvia made the rookie mistake of believing *everyone* was a prospect for what she offered. The reality is there is *no product or service* that appeals to *everyone*. And even if someone is in need of what you offer, she may not like you, may be unable to buy now, or may already work with a competitor.

Have a couple short illustrations you can share while networking that demonstrates positive outcomes your specific clients get from working with you or using your product. This allows prospects to self-identify if they have that need or know someone who might be interested in what you have, instead of assuming a need.

Have a compelling message. Sylvia was working hard. It was clear she came to the meeting to make the most of it. Trouble is she was chasing after *possible* prospects instead of attracting *ideal* prospects. She was missing a killer elevator speech!

To create a killer elevator speech, Veronika Noize, Head Coach at the DIY Marketing Center, says you need to have a seven- to nine-word phrase that distills the essence of who you help and the benefits they receive from working with you or using your product. It's the answer to the question, "What do you do?" It conveys who you are, how you help, and what *value* you bring to a specific segment of the marketplace.

Sylvia didn't set out to repel anyone while she was networking and she likely meant well. However, good intentions aren't enough if you want to attract great clients.

Use a P3 approach when networking. Network in places where you can meet your prospects, power partners, and peers. Identify where your target audience gathers and network there. Power partners are other business owners who serve the same market or industry, but with a noncompeting business. When you find someone with whom you really connect, create joint events or ways of cross promoting each other to help both of your businesses and your clients.

Some business owners are surprised when the suggestion is made that they network with peers. Meeting with your peers can provide you with greater insights into your industry through the sharing of ideas. It is also good to know what they do and who they serve to gain a different perspective. Even if a client isn't the right fit for you or you aren't able to meet a specific client deadline, it is good to know to whom you can confidently refer your prospect or client and know they will get their problem solved.

Have quality business cards on hand. This may seem basic, but we cannot tell you the number of times when after networking and asking someone for his or her business card, we're told he/she does not have one, or worse, has a homemade card that is very poorly laid out or printed. Your business card is a portable billboard for your company. Make sure it leaves a positive impression.

Be prepared to answer the question, "What's new with you?" If you are networking regularly and building relationships, chances are you'll run into people you already know. Introductions won't be necessary, but the person may ask how you are or what's new. Instead of talking about the weather or a sports team, be ready with something short you can share

about your business. It could be how excited you are about an upcoming class you are offering, an imminent new product launch, a client success, or a new piece of business you won. Remember, it's not a sales pitch, just a simple dialogue. Be sure to ask that person what is new with him.

Help introduce others. If you are a nervous networker, one of the easiest things to do is introduce someone new to the people you know at the event. It helps the newcomer feel welcomed and you look like a star. You will build trust and people will remember you—important elements to marketing and growing your business.

Really listen. There is nothing worse than talking with someone at a networking event and having him or her constantly looking over your shoulder to see who else is in the room. Look people in the eye, use active listening and body language to show understanding and engage in back and forth conversation. Even if your conversation lasts only for a few minutes, that is more effective than buzzing around the room collecting business cards. You may discover a way you can help that person (i.e., a resource you can send that person). Being a connector and resource to others is a great way to build relationships and remain on their minds.

Follow up. This is the most important step of networking. Meeting someone briefly at a mixer or association meeting a few times isn't going to build a deep relationship. Take time to call the people with whom you had a good connection. Set a time to meet for coffee to learn more about what they do, who they serve, and how they make referrals. Be prepared to share the same for your business. Find out how else you can help them and what resources you can share with them. Make an effort to stay in touch.

WARNING

- Just because you meet someone at a networking event and she gives you her business card does not give you permission to automatically add them to your newsletter list. Always ask first. See more about how to do this in the Email Marketing Campaigns section.

 NEXT STEPS

- Identify two or three places to network where you can meet your target market, potential power partners, and peers.

- Create a strong follow-up process after the networking event to build relationships and make the most of the time you spent networking.

- Keep track of the number of new potential clients you meet and how many times you have spoken to them for the purpose of gaining a meaningful relationship.

Open for Business

When I (Victoria) started my business in 2003, there was little fanfare. Just me at the computer working evenings and weekends to get her business started while working full time in corporate. Sure, I talked with a few friends and family members about what I was doing and attended periodic networking events through a local Chamber of Commerce. But few people knew I was open for business. Because I didn't have a brick-and-mortar storefront, I wasn't really sure how to get the word out.

Tell Them You Are Open

Whether you are opening the doors of a brand-new business, launching a product, or offering a new release, hosting an event or a grand opening is a terrific way to let your network and community know about your business, and create some buzz. This is an opportunity to connect with your current and past clients and engage your network. You are letting them know of something new and asking them to help you celebrate the achievement. Who doesn't love a party?

Host an Event

Marketing of your event will also help you connect with the local media and increase exposure about your business and increase traffic to your website. Have a clear goal and a desired outcome from this event. Is it to increase sales, add people to your list, encourage attendees to set up a time to talk with you, or something else? How well you do this can impact the trajectory of future sales.

Fast forward to 2012 when I rebranded and changed my business name. I was much more savvy and knew I wanted to host an open house to share the news and new service offerings with my clients and community. Because I work out of a home office, I didn't want to have a ribbon cutting at my home. Instead, I hosted a virtual open house. Since I have had clients across the country and even internationally and do much of my coaching by phone, this allowed me to include everyone in my event regardless of their geographic location. My goal for the event was to announce my business name change, grow my list, establish myself as an expert, and fill an upcoming virtual workshop.

The open house was a teleconference where I shared how to identify, address, and eliminate the three most common guilt stresses my market of women business owners face: money, marketing, and motherhood. It also included a brief preview of the programs I offered, and some of the success stories achieved by clients. This included having three of my clients live online to share their previous challenges, what they did with my help to resolve it, and the results they had achieved.

To add to the party atmosphere, I contacted several clients, colleagues, and strategic partners to ask if they would donate a prize I could give away during the virtual open house in exchange for including their business name in all of the event marketing. I ended up awarding over $1,500 in prizes from a variety of supporters locally and across the country. The prizes included gifts to educate women business owners as well as pamper them. Even if an attendee didn't win a prize, she walked away with a virtual swag bag of goodies!

Promotion of this virtual open house utilized a multistep and multichannel approach that included

- Mailed invitations

- A press release

- Postcards that could be handed out when networking

- An e-mail invitation to her newsletter list

- Phone calls to current and past clients and those in her network

- A blog article

- Several posts and tweets on social media (including LinkedIn, Facebook, and Twitter)

- Personal announcements everywhere she went.

During this 60-minute teleconference, a call to action was included. I shared valuable information, inspired my audience with stories of clients' successes, and provided participants with an opportunity to get their own help, support, and inspiration through an upcoming six-week online workshop. Through this event, I added several new names to my newsletter list, provided an engaging, informative, and fun tele-seminar, and had six paid registrants to the upcoming workshop. Because I had a strong follow-up process after the event and stayed in touch with the attendees and those new to my list, when I offered the paid workshop again six months later, the enrollment doubled!

Planning Your Event

Ideally, you will want to begin your planning six-eight weeks in advance. Start by deciding the reason for your event and what kind of event you want to have. This can be an in-person launch party, new product announcement, open house, or virtual event. Select a date and create a timeline of marketing strategies and tasks needing to be completed for your launch, working backwards from your event date. Be sure to include a variety of marketing strategies and channels to share the good news. If you have a physical location for your business, consider adding a ribbon cutting and inviting the local Chamber of Commerce. They will help promote your event and invite chamber members. Many of the local newspapers will send out a reporter to cover your event and take photos. Even if they don't, take your own and include them in your follow-up marketing and press release after the event.

Next Steps

- Decide what you need to announce and how you will do it.

- Create a plan for hosting your event.

- Use multiple marketing strategies to promote it.

- Implement a follow-up plan after the event to help move prospects one step closer to buying from or working with you.

- Track the number of attendees for your event(s).

Content Marketing

"What makes you the expert?" was the question posed to me (Stan) as the presenter spoke in front of the crowd. At that time I only had book knowledge without experience and I could speak from the examples of other authors, but had none to share of my own. My audience quickly departed.

What does this have to do with marketing? Audiences are becoming more and more sophisticated. They want more information than "here is my product, buy it." A good strategy for marketing is to focus on the top 5 -10 problems or challenges your market faces and why it is important to them to resolve them. This will provide you with content marketing topics that will be of interest to them and on which you can share solutions that will help.

What Is Content Marketing?

Content marketing enables you to be viewed by your audience as the expert with the purpose of attracting them to your company. This technique provides relevant and timely information without pushy sales. Many of the larger brands participate in studies, forums, and on regulation boards, which allows them to be seen as the leader in their industry.

Why Content Marketing Works

Many company decision makers prefer to get information about your company in a series of relevant meaty bundles, rather than a quick "punch you in the face" ad. Your consumers want to go down a 3journey with you and they don't want the story to wind up at a dead end. You must commit to content marketing as an ongoing strategy within your marketing plan.

New Concepts

You do not have to give away company secrets, but people like to know the next thing they can expect from you. When you are ready to disclose your prototype, it would be helpful to your audience to hear some solutions to issues they are facing. They do not want to hear solely about your product, rather they want the latest innovation in the area you are addressing.

Content Marketing Packaging

"You should do a video," people exclaimed to me. Another person proclaimed, "Podcast is the way to go." Yet another said a blog is the only method for content marketing. There are no silver bullets to this strategy. If you are not the best speaker, then a podcast may not be the right mechanism for you. Here are some other content marketing methods:

White paper. A white paper is a report on a product or service. This resource is used heavily within the STEM fields (science, technology, engineering, and mathematics) to explain breakthrough concepts. Hewlett-Packard wrote a free whitepaper entitled "Five Myths of Cloud Computing" to express an industry viewpoint. White Papers for Dummies by Graham Gordon (New York: Wiley, 2013), is a great resource.

News interviews. A pertinent conversation addressing current issues can be very engaging for potential clients and position you as an expert. Work with a marketing agency or media specialist to gain interviews with local newspapers, journals, magazines, or online venues. Resources like PR Newswire require a budget, but can take you step-by-step through the press release process. Apple always uses news interviews to communicate their new product.

eBooks. Content or a short report with examples and a deeper dive.

FAQs. Frequently asked questions that provide vital information to issues people face. These can be listed on your website, in your place of business, on a blog post, or in a document you provide to your customers.

Blog. Relevant timely information providing advice and solutions on a regular interval. 100 Best and Most interesting Blogs and Websites has a list that may fit you.

Newsletter or Website Article. Expert opinions from you or others regarding a relevant topic.

Video. Keep it under two minutes if you can. People like small snippets. You can have a few long videos with several short ones. Utilize Google Hangouts, your laptop camera, or smartphone to make short, informative videos on a budget. Hire a professional for a more polished result.

Podcast. Voice recording with great tips or insight from you. Keep these brief unless the topic requires it. Five minutes is a good size for regular recordings, but fifteen-, thirty-, and forty-five-minute formats are common and acceptable. Leverage tools like FreeConferenceCalling.com, WebEx, or Google Hangouts to create your voice recording. You can promote your podcast in iTunes.

Leverage Your Content

Once you have created content that is of interest to your market, relevant to their needs, and timely, you can share it through a variety of marketing channels. For example, I (Victoria) was interviewed via Skype for a podcast in which I shared strategies for connecting with my network and following up with prospects. The audio and video were recorded. The video could be used privately with clients while the audio could be transcribed and turned into an article or blog post. The same content could also be converted into a short seminar or webinar.

WARNING

- If you use content marketing as your method do not fall into the temptation of directly marketing your product. Your audience will be turned off if you mix sales with what should be considered expert information too often.

- Remember to mention your product or service, but do it in a way that contributes to the solution of a problem a client might face.

- Be real with your audience. Let them know you made mistakes and what you did to overcome any missteps. Audiences want to understand how you or your product or service will help them prevent issues they could face.

 NEXT STEPS

- Identify the top five problems of your ideal market.

- Determine what information you will share and create your first content marketing pieces

- Select one or two content marketing channels that align with your talents and abilities to add to your marketing plans. Track the size of your audience.

Remind

After this step, you will have invited your customer into your experience and provided solutions to bring them one step closer to purchasing.

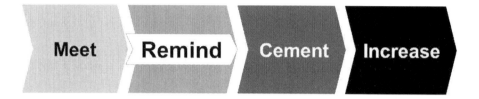

Press Releases

One of the most underutilized marketing tools many small business owners overlook is the press release. A press release is a written communication shared with the media about newsworthy information or announcements related to your business and market. The goal is to have media outlets pick up your story and publish information about it.

The key to a good press release is making it newsworthy. Advertising an upcoming sale of your products is not newsworthy. Writing about a problem your market has and how that problem can be solved by your product is newsworthy. Other reasons to write a press release include: an announcement of the grand opening of a business; an upcoming open house; a product launch or some other new release; an announcement of an award received; and upcoming special events.

When writing a press release, be very clear and concise. Keeping your information to one page is best, but two pages is the maximum length. The most important information, which answers the basic questions of journalism (Who? What? When? Where? How?), should be contained within the first two paragraphs. Include information to grab the reader's attention. Explain why the information is relevant and why they should care.

The best press releases read like an article and are written in the third person. Only use I or we when included in a direct quote. Including a provocative or eye-opening perspective on the topic can make your information stand out from the thousands of press releases the media receives. Present information of real value that prompts action like a visit to your website to learn more or registration for an upcoming event. Include a quote or two from the business owner or key individuals from your business or market commenting on this news. This brings a human element to your story.

The basic structure of a press release (see sample) includes:

- **FOR IMMEDIATE RELEASE** in a bold uppercase font at the very top.

- **An attention grabbing headline**—Keep it short and capitalize the first letter of each substantial word.

- **An optional subheading**—Do not repeat information already shared in the headline, but rather expand upon it. This should express a complete thought.

- **Location and date of the story**—Under the subheading type the city and state of the news and the full date of release (month, date, year).

- **News article**—The news article comes next and includes the most important information at the top. Use a 1.5 line spacing and ensure there are no misspelled words or grammar issues.

- **Company information**—One of your bottom paragraphs can include basic information about your company. This offers context for the reader.

- **END**—At the end of your news story, type the word END in all capital letters centered on the page. Right below it add ###. This lets the reader know this is the end of the information.

- **Company Contact Information**—Include the contact information for whomever a reporter should call if they wish to follow up or get additional details about your news.

Timing and Submittal of Your Press Release

It's important to get your press release out to the media in enough time for them to consider including the information in their publication. Verify with the media outlets to which you are sending your release what their specific deadlines are for publication. If sending a press release several weeks in advance of an event, you can send it again a couple weeks before the event as a reminder.

Additionally, the timing of your news in relation to what else is happening in the world needs to be considered. For example if you have a press release to send out and a major world event is occurring, it may be prudent to wait a few days or weeks before sending it. Sending press releases that are topical and relate to the current issues and world events can make them more relevant.

Uncomfortable writing your own press release? Look for a professional copywriter who can do it for you. Be sure to provide that person with all of the particulars of the news you wish to share.

Most media outlets prefer that press releases be submitted electronically. Check their websites or ask before you send your submission. A high resolution image accompanying your release may also make your news enticing for publication.

Press releases can be submitted to online sites like PRlog.org and PRNewswire.com. Some are free and others are fee based. In addition to online sites, consider also submitting to the local business editors for the newspapers and media outlets in your area. Your press release can also be sent to your local Chamber of Commerce (if you are a member), any associations to which you belong, and other industry-specific publications appropriate for the content presented.

It is important to build a relationship with the local editors and let them know you are there to support their work. Let them know the information for which you are an expert in case they ever need a quote or opinion on a story they are writing. Sending regular press releases (monthly) can also position you as an authoritative expert and keep you in the forefront with reporters.

Press Release Example

FOR IMMEDIATE RELEASE:

[Headline] Local Business & Marketing Coach Offering Webinar for The Hadley School for the Blind

[Location & Date] WINNETKA, IL – [News Article] Local Business & Marketing Coach Victoria Cook of The Center for Guilt-Free Success will offer the interactive webinar "How to Attract More Clients (and Business) with Three Magic Bullets of Marketing" through The Forsythe Center for Entrepreneurship (FCE), part of The Hadley School for the Blind's adult continuing education program. This webinar takes place on December 11th at 10 am CST as part of FCEs business and technology initiative designed to assist individuals who are blind or visually impaired in achieving their career goals.

During this webinar Cook will reveal three simple tools participants can use to make it easy for their best prospects to find them, and keep their favorite clients loyal. Participants will walk away from this presentation understanding the three critical phases of marketing, and how to handle each phase comfortably.

"Victoria's advice is practical and uses common sense: such as starting with what's in front of you, figuring out what you need and getting it and ignoring the need for perfectionism," said Colleen Wunderlich, Director, Forsythe Center for Entrepreneurship. "It is motivating to be shown how to work with what's already at your fingertips, and that process builds momentum towards the next steps."

Cook noted she is delighted to be presenting. "I'm thrilled to partner with FCE and The Hadley School for the Blind to bring proven marketing strategies to their community and help inspire entrepreneurs to start and grow their business."

The Center for Guilt-Free Success incorporates community, classes and coaching to help women entrepreneurs achieve success in their businesses. Using her simple, seven-step system, Cook helps her clients refocus their business and personal lives, and equips them with strategies to eliminate the guilt and increase profits.

The hour-long webinar training is December 11th from 10:00 – 11:00 am CST. Space at the event is limited, and those interested are encouraged to call Colleen Wunderlich at (847) 784-2889 or Victoria Cook at (847) 701-4739 to secure registration.

[Information about the company] For more information, visit the Center for Guilt-Free Success on Facebook at www.Facebook.com/Ctr4GFSuccess, the website at www.CenterForGuiltFreeSuccess.com or call 847-701-4739.

END

# # #

[Company Contact Information]

CONTACT:
Victoria Cook
The Center for Guilt-Free Success
Phone: 847.701.4739
Victoria@CenterForGuiltFreeSuccess.com
www.CenterForGuiltFreeSuccess.com

 **WARNING**

- Beware of writing a press release that is a sales pitch. That won't get published!

- Double check your press release and ensure there are no spelling or grammar errors

- Don't expect to send out a press release and it immediately generate business. A good press release shares information and invites the reader to learn more.

- Press releases can be expensive if you are hiring them out or having them submitted by a source so check the newsworthiness.

 **NEXT STEPS**

- Make a list of four or five newsworthy topics for which you can submit a press release.

- Decide if you will write a press release yourself or hire someone to do it for you.

- Make a list of the local news outlets in your area and obtain their contact information.

- Write and submit your first press release.

- Track the number of media outlets that picked up your press release.

The Consultation as a Marketing Tool

When I (Victoria) began my business, I was told that speaking is a great way for coaches to get clients. I like to speak and had a lot of information to share, so that sounded like a good fit to me. I created my initial talks complete with PowerPoint presentations and handouts. Then, at the end of my presentations, after just meeting these folks, I tried to sell them a $200—$300 coaching program. Now, most people wouldn't walk into a bar and ask the first single person they meet to marry them. Yet in a way, this was my approach when I tried to sell my coaching services. Needless, to say I didn't have too many takers and was left feeling frustrated.

The other strategy suggested to me for obtaining clients was to offer free coaching sessions. That's right—give away my time and expertise for free; help the prospect solve a problem so they will want more. That's what other professionals like doctors, lawyers, and accountants do, right? Uh . . . no. Free coaching often didn't work either. It enabled the prospect to move forward on her own while I was back to feeling frustrated.

So, what's a business owner to do? Well, first of all, remember that marketing is all about building relationships and the know, like, and trust factor. No one buys from someone he doesn't like or trust. Relationships take time to build and it is often said that it takes – seven to nine touches before someone buys. That is why newsletters, e-zines, follow-up phone calls, emails, etc. are important components to your marketing plans and strategies. But we are talking about sales here.

Lead Generation

The first rule of thumb is to draw prospects to you and make it easy for them to take another step towards purchasing your service or product. What can you offer your market that will have them self-selecting as a possible prospect for what you offer and raising their hand (metaphorically or literally) asking for more. This is called a *lead generator*.

When creating a lead generator, it is important to offer something of value to your market like a free report, an audio training, video presentation, eBook, limited free trial, introductory seminar, sample, low-cost consultation or checklist—just to name a few ideas. It's valuable enough for your prospect to exchange their contact information in order to receive the information you are sharing. (They are savvy and know that if they give out their information, you will market to them.). Then deliver the information promised. Now you have a warm prospect with which you can follow up and build a relationship.

Following Up

After delivering the information promised to your prospect, it's important to have a multistep process for following up with them. It can be a series of emails, a direct mail piece, phone call, handwritten note, letter, or a combination of them all (highly recommended). During the follow up, have another call to action to discuss their situation and identify next steps. This can be a low-cost assessment, diagnostic, or consultation.

The Consultation

Unlike the original advice I received, an initial assessment, diagnostic, or consultation is not a time for delivering your services or product for free. It is an opportunity to learn more about the prospect including but not limited to the following questions:

- What is the real challenge?

- What is their desired outcome?

- What have they already tried?

- What is currently working?

- What would they like to change?

- What kind of help or service are they looking for?

- What will be the benefit to them for solving these challenges?

- How motivated are they to make the changes needed to get their desired results?

- Is your product/service a good fit for them?

- What are the next steps they can take to move in the direction they seek?

This is an opportunity for business owners to do more listening than talking. Your prospects will tell you what they need and want. Your job is to look for alignment between what they need and what you offer. If there is alignment, then an offer of your product or service is your obligation. If there isn't alignment, suggestions of other resources or providers will leave a positive impression in the prospects' mind about you and your company (remember how business increased when Kris Kringle did that in the movie, *Miracle on 34th Street*) and they will remember you in the future.

I spoke with one prospect who was sure she needed the help of a coach and wanted to hire me. In the course of the consultation, I realized the prospect didn't need a coach. What she really needed was an organizer. I provided the prospect with a couple of names of organizers I knew and trusted that would help the prospect with the challenge she had. My prospect hired one of them and was thrilled with the results. She then went around bragging about me and how great my services were (even though she never hired me) and that even if I couldn't specifically help someone, I would refer prospects to the right resources. This increased my credibility and expertise in a group to which we both belonged that ultimately led to a paid speaking opportunity for me to the group.

Give It a Name

Nowadays just about every website and business card mentions the offer of a free consultation. Just because something is free does not mean prospects will jump at it. And sometimes those that do are not the right prospects. They may end up being folks who are "tire kickers" that just want some of your free time to get their questions answered and move on. That's why we don't recommend that business owners offer free consultations.

Instead, come up with a clever title for your consultation, identify the real benefits and takeaways from the session, and put a price on it. For example, call it a Business Breakthrough session, a Life Balance Assessment, or a Marketing Strategy Assessment. This will draw ideal prospects to you so you can offer something of great value to them and begin the relationship-building process. List that service on your website with a buy button. When following up with prospects, you can make a special offer on this session (discounted price, first five responders get a complimentary session) with an expiration date to create a sense of urgency and an appealing offer. This also provides a reason to follow up by phone to schedule a date for the prospect's session and help him or her take another small step towards working with you or buying your product.

Conducting Your Consultation

An initial assessment, diagnostic, or consultation can be 30–60 minutes in length and take place in person or by phone. Schedule it with your prospect just like any important business appointment. Send a confirmation email outlining:

- The purpose of the meeting
- The takeaways the prospect will get
- Instructions for the meeting (what number to call or where to meet)
- Questions you would like her to think about and send in advance of the meeting

- Expectations you have of him and what he can expect of you.

Next create a list of 10—12 open ended-questions that will help you assess the prospect's problem and desired outcome. The main purpose of this meeting is to understand the prospect, answer any questions she has about your company, product, or service, and identify resources/services that can help her. Ideally these resources/services will be something you offer. If they are, summarize your understanding of your prospect's need and present her with a couple options. See the Packaged Deals section for more details.

Following these strategies will attract prospects to you instead of you have to chase after them.

WARNING

- Beware of giving away too much during your consultation or trying to solve the prospect's issues during the meeting. The consultation is about showing that you understand the prospect's problem or concern and are willing to help that person decide what next step he or she will take to resolve the problem.

NEXT STEPS

- Brainstorm lead generation ideas of value to your market.
- Decide what kind of consultation you can offer.
- Name the consultation and outline the benefits and takeaways for your prospect.
- Add this to your website and follow-up process.
- Track the number of people who called or accepted your consultation.

Packaged Deals

Service providers often fall into the trap of pricing their services by the hour. This type of pricing can be intimidating to the client and cause them to constantly evaluate if they are getting their money's worth. It also requires they make multiple buying decisions every time additional products or services are needed. Conversely, selling products/services in a package is not only better for a business owner's cash flow, it also helps clients stay committed, get the desired results, and increases their level of satisfaction in the product or service purchased.

Four good reasons to provide packaged deals for your clients*** include the following:

1. To reduce your prospects' fears about money

2. To demonstrate your expertise

3. To help you (and your prospects) visualize how you can work together

4. To show the scope of your service to your prospects.

Some key elements to remember about packaged deals*:

1. Names can give packaged deals an emotional impact, so be sure that the name reflects what the clients want from the process.

2. Stop giving it away! Develop an introductory packaged deal that includes a review, assessment, or a "taste" of your services or a small sample size of your product, and charge for it. Give away what doesn't cost you money (so you can be very generous). For example, a report, recorded webinar, or introductory class, etc., but do not

---

* Information from *Marketing Blueprint Workshop* by Veronika Noize. Copyright © 2002. Used by permission of the author. All rights reserved by the original author.

work for free. Teach your client to value and respect your time, or find clients that already do. Understand that an initial consultation is not really an opportunity for service, but a sales meeting in which you determine need, fit, and strategies for moving forward to achieve the client's objective.

3. Upgrades, extensions, and additional services can turn an inexpensive packaged deal into a very profitable one. Have a menu of services that your clients can use to upgrade their experience with you.

4. Allow for a certain amount of customization within your packaged deals. This can be as simple as a choice of A or B, X or Y, and 1 or 2. Two or three small decisions/options equal a "customized" package for your clients, which will enhance their experience and satisfaction.

Create programs and packaged deals that help your market to solve their problem(s). For example, a business offering web development services might include a low-cost introductory website assessment. This will facilitate a deeper understanding of the prospects' current and future needs.

The business owner can then recommend one of three packaged deals: (1) A mobile-ready starter package with five basic pages; (2) a business package that includes options in the starter package plus ten additional web pages, a blog, search engine optimization, and photo gallery; and (3) a premium package that includes everything in the first two packages, plus embedded video, up to 25 pages with training on how to manage the site. The middle package will be priced attractively to entice purchases.

Minimize the Risk

Consider ways in which you can reduce the prospect's fears of buying and make it easier for him to say yes. This might include a money-back guarantee, 90-day warranty, try-before-you-buy samples, free replacements, or an easy-cancel policy.

 WARNING

- Be sure the program or package you offer is really something your prospects want and not just something you want to sell. A great package offering a solution no one wants will not be of benefit to you or your prospects.

 NEXT STEPS

- Identify the results your prospects want and create a program or package that provides the solution.

- Offer a risk reversal to reduce any barriers for prospects to buy.

- Track the number of packaged deals and measure the success.

Cement

After you complete this step, you will solidify the relationship with your customer base and your role as the expert.

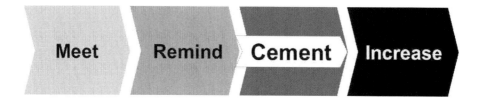

Keeping in Touch

"We ought to do a newsletter" were the naive words spoken by a volunteer organization to me, who I (Stan) served as the marketing chair and wondered why we needed a newsletter. The answer was "everyone else does this, we should too." We were doomed to failure, because we had no purpose.

Start with a Purpose

Newsletters can be very powerful if leveraged the right way. If you are communicating to a group of bubblegum card collectors, they want to hear the latest about their craft. The problem that many people fall into is they want to push their information on the group so the bubblegum card collector has to sift through your noise about how great your company is, rather than giving me what I'm looking for.

Relevance versus Date

Writing a newsletter because it is *time* to write the newsletter is never a good reason for news. The recipient wants *quality,* timely information regarding his or her subject of interest. You are supposed to be the expert, so your followers will seek your advice for something relevant. If you cannot sustain relevant information on a weekly basis, then maybe you should cut back your frequency to a time frame where the information can be timely yet not forgotten.

Choose a Good Frequency

Weekly newsletters are great when dealing with a crowd focused on a crisis. In fact daily news can be digested for some situations where pertinent instructions need to be carried out with goodwill messages mixed in. I worked as a volunteer for forest fire relief. My followers needed instructions on how to deliver food and relief to the firefighters and they wanted some good news about who was rescued on a daily basis. On the other hand, seasonal newsletters can be use for the spring, summer, autumn, and winter festivals.

A Picture Is Worth a Thousand Words

Pictures wake up a newsletter. Add poignant words with an eye-catching picture and you will have a higher open rate for that article. In fact articles with pictures have a 75% higher open rate than those without.

Be Brief

We saw a news article with nothing but words. It made us tired just looking at it! These days people spend about 10 - 20 seconds per article and they pick and choose which information in your article is relevant to them. Break your information into bite sized chunks and link people to other places who need a deeper set of instructions or understanding.

Think 82/20 where 80% is industry related updates or something of interest to your reader and 20% can be reserved for upcoming events and new services for your company.

WARNING

- Do not start a newsletter because you think you need one.

- Stay away from the temptation of focusing too much on sales in your articles.

- Do not drone on and on. Get to the point.

- Only send newsletters according to the CAN-SPAM 2014 rules.

 NEXT STEPS

- Understand your audience and meet their ongoing needs.

- Choose a great headline for your relevant topic to increase your open rate.

- Identify relevant or thought-provoking pictures or icons to break up text.

- Start with a broader frequency and add more intervals as needed.

- Include a call to action for each part of the newsletter. For example, Click here to learn more or Join us for the event.

- Track the articles read by your followers to measure success.

Email Marketing Campaigns

At first I Stan did not know what an email marketing campaign was, so I opened up email, wrote a note to my friends and family letting everyone know I was in business. My "do it yourself" pride crashed to the ground when I tried to hit send and it would not go. A message "Too Many Recipients" doused my flame, but did not squelch it. I told myself, "I will simply have to send multiple emails." After spending a large amount of time breaking apart the list, my DIY pride returned. The next day I sat next to a very silent phone, so I checked my email. I had a couple of replies, one inviting me to a party and the other was a relative who hadn't heard from me in a while.

Regular Email Is Limited

I called my email company to troubleshoot why my emails didn't go through and I was told I could only send to a list of 250 people at a time I also had more bad news. Many people did not like receiving an email with "Read Receipt" turned on so there went my idea of collecting any statistics on my campaign. Regular email cannot perform like an email marketing service.

Email Marketing Campaign Parts

At one time I thought an effective email was one where I told "everything." This way I could say, "I said it in the email." This is far from the truth when developing an email campaign. The average person wants to spend 10 seconds or less to read your entire email. My company, Honor Service Office Email Software, recommends the following:

- **Compelling Email Subject.** This has to be compelling enough to make the customer open the message without it ending up in the spam folder (i.e., "Here's a Quick Way to Develop Apps" or "7 Secrets to the Hidden Job Market").

- **Headline.** Tell the reader what he will see and read but make your statement effective enough to stand alone. ("Reduce Conflict by 50% in Your Department" says it all.)

- **Pictures.** Use professional or stock photos to develop a campaign with fewer words and more pictures. Picture emails are opened and forwarded 70% more than all text-only messages.

- **Email Body.** Write a short compelling, purposeful, action-oriented statement in summary fashion.

- **"Call to Action" Link.** "Learn More" or "Click Here" Link to your website or a location of interest.

Email marketing companies include Constant Contact, Mail Chimp, or Honor Services Office.

Open Rates Tell a Lot

When I sent my first email campaign through a paid service, I saw the stats roll in and I was highly disappointed! I mean only 50% of the people opened the note that I had meticulously designed! Little did I know that the open rate average across all industries is only 22%. This takes into account hard and soft bounced emails.

Rules for Campaigns. Some rules about email campaigns should not be ignored. Federal rules require the following for commercial email:

- **Identification.** The email must be clearly identified as a solicitation or advertisement for products or services.

- **Opt-Out.** The email must provide easily-accessible, legitimate, and free ways for you to reject future messages from that sender.

- **Return Address.** The email must contain legitimate return email addresses, as well as the sender's postal address.

Make sure you get permission to send communication to your audience. Send an email campaign that asks permission to keep sending emails.

Be engaging when you send your opt-in campaign. Offer a free book or a large discount on your product. People will not opt-in for nothing especially if they do not know you very well.

Look for the FCC Guidelines site: http://www.fcc.gov/guides/spam-unwanted-text-messages-and-email

Clean Up Your Email Lists

It is vital that you keep your email lists as up-to-date as possible. Check to see if all of the email addresses on your list are valid and have opted into your list. Some email validation/cleanup sites include DataValidation.com, BriteVerify.com, or LeadSpend.com.

Avoid Spam Words

My desire to get people to open the email campaign made me think of clever email titles that would entice people to open the message. This was stressful! Little did I know I had fallen into a trap many people discover: I developed a "spammy" title and my message wound up in the spam folder. Therefore, most people did not get my message.

- Do a search for spam words to avoid and you will get numerous lists of words to stay away from.

- Be sincere rather than gimmicky.

- Get permission. People mark email as spam because the sender has not asked them if they could send email on a regular basis.

Hire a Professional

If it doesn't look good, it will be marked as spam. Amateurish email campaigns with too many words, bad formatting, and horrible pictures will quickly be dismissed by your intended audience. They will mark it as spam and the money you saved doing it yourself will be lost because of the mass retreat from your list.

Click-Thru Rates

Your call to action link will be important as this is one of the main stats to show the success of your campaign. The picture along with brief words should compel your audience to click through your campaign. Make sure the landing page is up to date with fresh information.

Frequency/Duration

"You are bugging me!" are words of death from your audience to whom you have sent too many email campaigns. Some people say "more is a good thing," but sending email campaigns to the same audience reaches a law of diminishing returns. After the first few emails, people will turn you off if the next are not timely or relevant to their need. Also, good stats happen in the first few days of your campaign. Many people take up to a week to open emails, but rarely beyond two.

WARNING

- Do not send an email campaign without sending an opt-in campaign.

- Watch out for spam words in your email title and body.

- Be professional, otherwise your campaign will be marked as spam or you could lose your audience.

 NEXT STEPS

- Clean up your lists regularly.

- Hire a professional to do your marketing campaign.

- Use pictures to describe your service and fewer words.

- Sell one thing at a time if possible.

- Track open, click-thru, and unsubscribe rates.

Increase

After this step, you will have prepared the items to increase the awareness, visibility, and loyalty of your customer base.

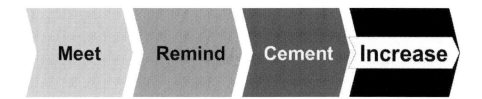

Social Media Business Pages

Early Facebook provided a page where I (Stan) could do business, but I would get interrupted with friends who wanted me to plant corn on their virtual farm. This seemed like a waste of time. I would hear stories of lore where others would get huge amounts of business from tweeting or through Facebook.

I jumped right in, established my Facebook business page, invited family and friends and had nothing to say. I nervously posted things about my business and a few people liked what I said, but I received no business. I was dying on the vine quickly. What could I say? Was I using this social thing correctly?

Social media can be a helpful tool to your marketing. We suggest small business owners leverage social media as a relationship building tool to keep conversations going with your audience/community. What that means is only show up on the social media networks that are important to your community. Specifically, stay focused on just a couple of social media channels and make sure to stay in conversational contact. Be sure to respond to comments.

One of the best ways to leverage social media is to create a map of information to share and obtain through this strategy. This can include

- Information about your company, service, or product

- Announcements you want to make

- Questions you want to ask your market

- Feedback you would like from your market

- Non-confidential news about clients

Depending on who your community is, you will have a different type of page: business page, personal page, or group page (where you and your audience can have a dynamic conversation with each other). I (Victoria) have a women's business development group that has a private group page. It's not just about posting a bunch of advertising. They engage in real conversations where people ask questions and get answers. This level of dialogue can be very difficult to do on a business page. Not only is a group page helpful to the members of the community, it can also be very lucrative to the business owner facilitating the conversations and sharing information with members.

Quite frankly social media isn't just free marketing like it used to be. It's a nice way to get people engaged and build relationships. Social media is really all about the relationship.

Here is some high level information about the various social media platforms and how best to utilize them for small business owners.

Facebook and Google+ Business Page

Facebook is the 900-pound gorilla of the social media world. With over 1 billion subscribers, it cannot be ignored in your social media mix. Google + is steadily adding more and more small business to its world. The more you appear on Google, the higher up on the search your business appears. Volumes of books could be written on this topic alone but we will break this page down to a few quick tips.

Utilize the Cover Photo Areas. In the banner include a professional depiction of your business with hopefully some creativity and inspiration.

Logo. Rectangle logos out, square in. Keep it simple.

Newsfeed Posts. This is where you get your audience's attention. Fresh content from you or other pages you follow draws people to return to your page. Remember to make only post about 20% about yourself. Use big bold pictures and captivating, relevant stories. Ask questions, share client success stories or testimonials, request feedback, and share other relevant information. Be shareable. That is the way to grow your reach.

Photos. Pictures of your product, service, or you in action connects the audience to your progress.

Video. Show the audience how to use your product or service or share tips and information. Keep it short.

Facebook/Google + Stats. Likes (or +1's), views, total reach, post reach, comments and clicks are all measures of engagement on Facebook. Make sure you provide compelling content mixed in with scheduled product offerings to measure the success of your marketing campaign.

Change up. Switch identities to post and comment on Facebook or Google + pages while you are logged in as your business page name by clicking on the identity icon at the top of the page (looks like a small, upside down triangle). Like other pages and ask for a reciprocal response. Check out the newsfeed while you are in your business identity and you will see business feeds of the pages you liked that you can share.

Don't ignore your own content. Go to your business page under your own identity and share the content to your personal page and any groups to which you belong. Be sure to like posts on your business page and make comments on them as yourself. Tagging friends and clients in the comments can draw others into the conversation. Just don't overuse this feature.

LinkedIn Business Page

LinkedIn is definitely a powerhouse in the business world. If yours is a business-to-business model (B2B) then you must have a LinkedIn business page. Be interesting, but remember: your audience is very professional. Include video, photos, and explanations of your product or service similarly to Facebook. The difference is if your company hosts a LinkedIn discussion group, then that can be tied to your business page for content marketing.

LinkedIn Stats. Impressions, clicks, interaction, and engagement.

Twitter Business Page

Brevity is Twitter's mantra. A quick note or tweet about your event or new offering of great content you just found is welcome in this medium. Link it to your Facebook and LinkedIn pages so audiences can follow you and gain new insights about your business. Images can be used to enhance your message and increase the likelihood of being read and retweeted.

Great Content to Share

Your customers are looking for engagement, offerings, and information. Retailers are just now getting to the place where special deals and coupons are strictly on social media. Make sure you share your posts with your audience to show up on your personal newsfeed. Facebook and LinkedIn use *share*; Twitter uses retweet and Google Plus uses *+1 to share*. Keep content relevant to your audience.

Examples of Content Marketing

- Feature Your Client. Create a write up on a client and others will gain satisfaction from this person.

- Limited Time Offerings. Post LTO deals sporadically to keep people coming back.

- Polls. Post a short poll to draw people to your page and engage your audience.

- Your Own Product. Now that you have posted some great content, format information about your business in the same content-like fashion. Your customers will appreciate this.

WARNING

- Do not mistake social media stats as business growth stats. Your product or service business metrics are stronger indicators of business health.

- Do not mix social interaction with business. Keep your personal social media pages separate.

 NEXT STEPS

- Identify the top social media channels to connect with your market.

- Set up the business pages on each of the social media platforms.

- Track the metrics on all social media platforms.

Advertising

Sitting by the radio, I (Stan) waited for his advertising spot to play. The station did a great job with the music, recording quality and voice-over choice. When I heard my spot play, I was elated. I stared at the phone and it didn't ring. "Maybe my phone is out of order," I thought. I checked my website stats and had no visits. Then I remembered the sales person's words: "You will need a lot more segments in order to make this ad campaign effective."

Why Advertise?

Advertising is a quick way for a large audience to hear about your product or service. Advertising is more than visibility or pushy sales. It is about invoking credibility and trust in your product or brand. It also is a guide to a process that leads to the point of purchase.

Depending on the advertising channel you choose, placing an ad can be quite expensive. Television and radio stations require a budget of about $10,000 and above to even begin leveraging an ad campaign's effectiveness.

Advertising Expectations

If like me you have expectations of what you'd like your ad campaign to do, you might want to take a realistic view of what's in store. Placing an ad in a prominent magazine doesn't mean you will be flooded with new prospects. Small results could mean great results. Here are a few ways to monitor your expectations:

Set Realistic Capture Rate (Conversion Rate) Goals. Are you sitting down? Great ads yield a 1% to 2% capture rate according to a very large Quick Service Restaurant (QSR). For every 100 people who hear about your product or service, you may only convert one or two. This does not mean advertising is ineffective.

It may mean your audience isn't ready to purchase from you the first time they hear about you. Some of the skeptics may want to wait and see. How many new customers will purchase your product the first time they hear about it?

Think of Step Conversions. Some people are ready to purchase and some need to take one step closer to you. Step conversion has the person sign up for more information or some other action that will bring them one step closer to the point of purchase.

Include a Call to Action. Using "Call now" for a radio ad or *Click Here to Purchase* or *Buy Now* for a print ad might sound direct, but they are guides that remove ambiguity for your customer.

Where to Advertise

Free ads sound great but are very hit or miss. First, ask yourself, "Where does my market live?" Does your market live in groups that meet regularly? Are there online get-togethers? Here are a few places to consider:

Group Sponsorship Ad. This costs less than mass media and can be an effective way to advertise to your target audience. Selling to raincoat engineers through the raincoat engineer council increases the likelihood of someone being interested.

Social Media Ad. When you look to the right side of your screen, you can see several ads that are selected based on your interests. Facebook, Twitter, LinkedIn and Google have developed great methods of advertising and easy-to-create ads. But are they right for you? Consider . . .

- **Click Thru.** You're charged your bid amount for *every* click. If you bid $1 per click, then that's what you are charged. The upside is you can get some great metrics immediately; the downside is that fraudulent clicks can occur (competitors; spammers).

- **Impression.** You're charged for the number of appearances your ad makes, depending on how much you bid and who else makes a bid at the time. Depending on your bid, your ad can be shown a lot or not at all. Sometimes click-thru rates still apply.

Newsletter Ad. Newsletter advertising is quite popular. Depending on the quality of the newsletter, you can reach your target audience. If a power partner (someone serving a similar client market as you with a non-competing product or service) has a large and responsive list, buying ads in their newsletter can be a wise investment.

Partnership Website Ad. Your website is your best advertising and you gain credibility by advertising on a site with high credibility. High traffic sites are a great source of impressions.

High-End Ad. Billboard, radio, and television spots are high end, because if leveraged correctly, your product or service will be seen by an extremely large audience. The costs are very high, so consult with a professional before choosing any of these. Gross Rate Points (GRPs) can add up depending on market size, time of day, and number of times shown.

What to Say

Keep your ad brief. Advertising is not your life story; rather, it is an appetizer to bring people to the meal. Plan your advertising carefully before finalizing your ad. Mistakes are never forgiven, so have someone proofread your work. Cheap, overplayed catchphrases are dangerous. Be genuine and compelling. Also, consider the benefits of your product or service, rather than focusing on a hard sell.

Budget for Your Ad

Before you start advertising, set your overall marketing budget. This should be about 10% to 12% of gross annual sales. Calculate your operating expenses, and be careful not to let the advertisers sell you on a hard and fast percentage for your business.

Calculate what the true markup cost of your product or service will be to cover the marketing. Calculate labor and other expenses and determine your profit. From there maximize your advertising dollars to generate sales. Advertising could be anywhere from 2% to 7% of your gross sales.

WARNING

- Stay within your budget. Advertising can be costly and should be done with some regularity. Budget out a year versus a one-time shot.

- Set low expectations on free channels of advertising. These can be effective if a lot of effort is put behind them.

- Setting a brief exposure point is not an effective strategy. Think frequency or long term. It takes a while before your brand sinks in to the masses.

- Don't hide behind advertising! Your business pages and ads should provide an opportunity for you to engage your audience.

 NEXT STEPS

- Decide if advertising is the correct strategy for your business.

- Find where your audience lives and budget for your ad to reach this target.

- Hire a professional. Amateur ads waste money.

- Execute sales along with marketing and advertising.

- Alternate advertising channels and pay attention to the length of time your ad can remain effective. The same old ad will be ignored after a while.

Second 30 Days Implementation Checklist

Meet

- ☐ Read the Second 30 Days section to get an overview.
- ☐ Identify two or three places to network and meet prospects, power partners, and peers.
- ☐ Create a strong follow-up process for after networking to build relationships.
- ☐ If opening a new business or launching a new product or service, decide on how to announce it.
- ☐ Create a plan and follow up for next launch using multiple strategies.

Remind

- ☐ Make a list of four or five newsworthy topics on which to submit press releases.
- ☐ Identify local and/or national news outlets and contact information for submitting your press releases.
- ☐ Write (or have written) a press release and submit it.
- ☐ Create a list of topics for content marketing pieces.
- ☐ Plan a publishing schedule for upcoming content marketing, social media and press releases.
- ☐ Brainstorm lead generation ideas of value to your ideal market.
- ☐ Decide what kind of consultation to offer and outline the benefits and takeaways for the prospect.
- ☐ Outline consultation follow-up process.

☐ Review top five challenges of your ideal market and create a program or packaged deals to solve the ideal market's problems.

☐ Draft a lead generation tool.

☐ Add consultation name and takeaways to website.

Cement

☐ Select a client relationship management tool for tracking contacts and sending a newsletter.

☐ Decide the frequency for a newsletter.

☐ Create a newsletter template.

☐ Compile a newsletter with thought-provoking pictures, relevant information, and calls to action.

Increase

☐ Select one or two content marketing channels the ideal market uses to share the content.

☐ Set up complete profiles on the selected social media platforms.

☐ Decide if advertising is the right strategy for reaching the market and create a budget.

☐ Have a professional ad created if applicable.

☐ Select key performance indicators to track and assess marketing success or areas of improvement.

send a note   reach out

they want to hear from you

contact

email them

your

customers

call them

call her   call him

Third 30 Days—Follow-Up Phase

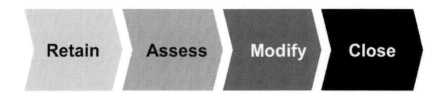

client rewards

CRM

loyalty programs

referrals

are cool

follow up

keep them coming back

lead generators

make it easy

incentives

Retain

After completing this step, you will have the tools in place to keep your market coming back for more and sending others your way.

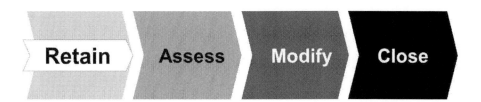

Following Up to Retain Growth

In October of 2009, I (Victoria) searched for a way to engage my e-zine list and generate business. I had the idea of creating and offering a 30-day goals challenge e-course. Registrants received an email from me every day for 30 days with information, resources, and encouragement to complete one small goal in the next 30 days. It was a terrific lead generator, but what made it successful and beneficial to my business was having a strong follow-up process.

After prospects registered for the program, they immediately received a welcome email and information about what was offered through the program, including a debriefing session at the end of the 30 days to discuss what worked, what didn't, and what was next. This session was to help participants maintain their momentum (or get back into action) and continue achieving their goals, and an opportunity for a sales conversation if the prospect needed more help and support. Additional follow-up steps were conducted at specific intervals, including a phone call to welcome the prospect and schedule a debriefing session, a quick-start tele-class, inspirational video messages, and the actual debriefing phone session.

During the initial 32 days of the challenge launch, I added 59 people to my list from 20 different states, two Canadian provinces, and five countries abroad, including Brazil, Russia, Germany, Scotland, and the UK. Twenty-four percent of the registrants took advantage of the debriefing session and 43% of them were converted into a brand-new group coaching program I offered. It also led to my first international private coaching client. Comparing my income for the months of October 2009 and January 2010, I experienced a 66% increase. I continued offering the challenge and following up with prospects in 2010. Overall comparing my yearly income for 2009 and 2010, I earned 60% more in 2010 as a direct result of the 30-Day Challenge and follow-up process utilized.

Remind Your Customer

Business owners most often don't follow up with prospects and clients because they don't want to appear pushy. They falsely believe that if they let clients and prospects know through advertising, email, or a direct mail piece what product or services they offer, and the clients or prospects are interested, they will contact them to buy. However, with all the demands on a person's time, even if he sees an ad for something he's interested in purchasing, he can easily forget about it. Following up is a way of helping a prospect or client take a desired next step. It is not uncommon when contacted by phone, that a prospect will thank the business owner for calling, because registering for the class or taking advantage of the special offer was something she wanted to do, but just hadn't yet made the time to do so.

Use Variety

To avoid feeling like the pushy salesperson when following up, use a variety of strategies including, but not limited to email, phone call, postcard, handwritten note, letter campaign, video message, or direct message through social media. Decide on an interval timeline for your follow-up steps. A strong client relationship management tool (CRM) (such as Honor Services Office) can help track your process and generate a to-do list to keep you on track. Automate your follow-up process where you can, using your CRM, auto-responders, and social media aggregator (such as Hootsuite or TweetDeck) to schedule social media contact messages.

WARNING

- Don't limit follow-ups to just one strategy (e.g., phone calls). Business owners can feel pushy and prospects can feel stalked.

- Be consistent with your process. Each step builds on the next and consistently executing the process creates momentum.

 NEXT STEPS

- Identify the follow-up process for your lead generator(s).

- Use a CRM Tool like Honor Services Office to keep track of prospects and get reminded to follow up.

- Create and use your follow-up process.

- Track the progress to identify areas of improvement and which parts of your process work best.

Loyalty and Referral Programs

"How do I bring customers back more often?" was a problem that was posed to me (Stan) from a small business owner who worked in the quick service restaurant industry. We discussed what worked and found that several other restaurant business owners had implemented their own makeshift loyalty programs.

After testing the concept in a large number of restaurants, it was found that the program increased loyalty by 10%, but was expensive because too much food was given away. This made us retool the program to give away premium items to customers who had a large number of visits so we added tiers to the program.

Once you have taken the time to acquire and convert a client, it's important to take great care of them so they stick around. It is also less expensive to market to existing clients than it is to acquire a new one. Instead of deep discounting to retain customers, here are some strategies to reward referral and purchasing behaviors.

Loyalty Program

One way to ensure that clients and customers stick around and continue purchasing from you is to have a loyalty program, something that rewards ongoing purchases. Have you ever had a punch card to your favorite coffee house, sandwich shop, or nail salon? Make ten purchases and the eleventh one is free. It keeps you coming back in anticipation of getting your next purchase free. Here are some key components of an effective loyalty program:

- **Program Name**. Since loyalty programs are very commonplace, give yours a name to make it fun. For example perhaps you run the "Top of the Heap" program for the person who adds the most pizza toppings.

- **Rewards.** Rewards can include a free item of whatever they have purchased or a complimentary product or service that will be of benefit to them.

- **Interval.** Define the periods your loyalty program will run. Is it ongoing or for a finite time? Will you use punch cards? For example, some coffeehouses punch your loyalty card a number of times before you get a free cup of coffee. The cost is minimal and spurns more visits. Will you have a magnetic stripe card program?

- **Extended Benefactor.** One would think the only benefactor has to be your customer and you. But the program could also be extended to bring others in. For example, you could give away two tickets to a ball game instead of one. One ticket for the benefactor (initial loyalty participant) and a second one for the additional participant. This will require that the additional participant to sign up for the program as well.

Metrics. Metrics are key to any loyalty program. Calculate how much you have given away versus new or repeat business. Keep those punch cards or coupons or write down how much you have given and total it at the end of the day.

Referral Program

An ideal client is one who is so happy with your product, service, information, or experience that he or she tells everyone. Satisfied clients attract satisfied potential clients, and they can become your unpaid sales team, which in turn lowers your new client acquisition costs. The program should be easy to use and rewarding. Here are some components to consider when developing a referral program:

- **Program Name.** Enable your customers to have a sense of belonging to something. By giving your program a name, you can spark your customers into driving more customers through your doors. For example, "Lose 20 in 30 Program" could have referral components that not only help the customer lose 20 pounds in 30 days, but he will be motivated to invite others.

- **Structure.** Will this be a straight referral, where for every referral received you give the customer something, or will you have tiers to your program? With tiers, both parties win if they work hard together. For example, you may have a basic tier which rewards something small, a middle tier which rewards something of greater value and an upper tier which rewards at an extreme level, but requires a larger amount of new customers or revenue.

- **Incentive.** Cash always speaks clearly and everyone wants some of the action, but do you always have to give up cash? Not necessarily. You can motivate the referral participants with reduced or free products and services or gifts your power partners are willing to offer. Whatever the incentive, be consistent so the program will catch on.

- **Program Compensation Period.** When will you give your customer his or her compensation? Rewarding your customer every time he or she brings in someone new can be cumbersome. Put conditions around the referral. For example, pay when the new customer purchases a certain dollar amount of goods and services.

- **Program Rules and Instructions.** Be clear about the incentives, compensation period, eligibility and program structure. Remember, you are in business and the program is an incentive, not your primary business.

- **Tracking Mechanism.** Tracking the success of your program is extremely important. How many new customers signed up or how much product was sold because of the referral? Did you receive a return on your investment? Calculate the overall costs by totaling the incentives given out plus any other related expenses.

Ongoing Communication

People want to hear how you are doing, who you have helped, and what's new within your company. We've already mentioned email marketing and newsletters in other chapters, but there are other ways to keep your following abreast of what you are doing.

- **Call Them.** Pick up the phone and ask, "How are you doing?" Be genuine.

- **Write Them.** A note or paper newsletter is more likely to be read than email these days.

- **Visit Them.** Depending on your business, visit your customer base regularly. Be visible.

Tell them about your journey, an issue you are resolving, upcoming events, new releases, special offers, or members-only news and resources. There is a lot to choose from. Using these three strategies will have clients feeling special, rewarded, and loyal.

 WARNING

- Be careful of offering discounts as a retention strategy. This can backfire into a "discount only" purchase pattern.

- Monitor your loyalty program to prevent theft and counterfeiting.

- Loyalty and referral programs can be expensive, so design them well and continually monitor your ROI.

 NEXT STEPS:

- Identify the interval of purchases you wish to reward and create a loyalty program.

- Start small with your loyalty and referral program and increase the size annually.

- Decide on the loyalty rewards and referral incentives that enable ROI.

- Decide on what kind of client communication vehicle(s) you will use, and at what intervals they will be sent. Communicate to your client base now.

marketing plan

manage time

pr campaign

email marketing

put it all
together

we honor and serve you

advertise

be guilt-free

consultation

newsletter

Assess

After completing this step, you will understand the key performance indicators from the metrics of your marketing campaign as input to making changes to your approach.

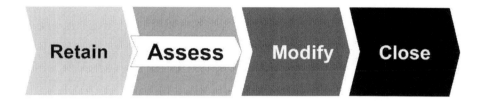

Dealing with Marketing Setbacks

As Stan shared in a previous chapter, he was very excited about advertising his executive resume business on the radio. With his budget spent and the realization that he was not attracting ideal clients, he could easily have thrown in the towel. Instead, he recognized that the strategy was sound, but the execution needed a bit of fine-tuning.

Marketing is often a series of tests. Test a strategy to see how it works for your business and how it is perceived by your market. While it can be disappointing to not get the desired results, much can be learned.

Take a Step Back and Look

When faced with a marketing setback, it is helpful to step back and look at the situation as objectively as possible. To do this, it may be helpful for you to ask yourself a series of questions including these:

- *What worked?* You can always see what went wrong, and you can certainly review that next. However, start with uncovering what worked even a little bit.

- *What were some of the positive results?* You may find the results were good, but for a different area of your business.

- *Did the message resonate with my audience?* If the marketing resulted in feedback or contact from prospects, review what was said or asked. Did it relate to your offer? If not, perhaps the message was unclear for your market.

- *Did I target the right segment?* Was the message right, but aimed at the wrong segment or presented through the wrong channel?

- *Was the offer of strong interest to my market?* Ask some of your key clients or prospects what they need and want to see if your offer aligned with their needs.

- *Did I give this strategy enough time to really work?* Most strategies and tactics need a minimum of 90 days to show progress. Some need longer.

- *What needs to be done for this marketing strategy, tactic, or campaign to get better results?* Talk with your team, clients, and prospects to see how they feel about it. You may find that the offer was of interest, but the price point or timing was off.

Handling Mistakes

Sometimes business owners move a bit too fast and mistakes happen. Instead of putting *$50 off* on your campaign, you accidentally put *$500 off* in your marketing campaign. Respond immediately and apologize for the inconvenience. Offer something for the customers' inconvenience. Be upfront.

Dealing with Bad Reviews

Despite doing the very best we can to provide excellent products or top-notch service, not everyone is going to be happy with the results. Those customers are often the ones who are quick to post a review. Having someone say less-than-flattering things about you and your business certainly stings. But how this is handled will speak volumes about who you are, and the kind of business you run. Don't avoid controversy. Handle the issue with transparency.

One family-owned food establishment struggled to see any less-than-perfect reviews from customers. Because they took the feedback personally and could not respond without getting emotional, they decided to ignore all the reviews and not solicit any further reviews, even from happy customers. Over time, this resulted in a poor rating that ended up costing them a very large corporate party that scheduled a reservation until one of the executives noticed their rating.

Sometimes, in spite of all your hard work, someone will provide a bad review. Here's what you can do when you face a review:

- **Regularly check reviews.** Set aside time each week to check your social media channels where clients can leave reviews to keep abreast of your online reputation.

- **Respond to and thank reviewers promptly.** Even if the review is less than what you desire, it is important that you respond quickly. Thank the person for taking the time to share his or her experience.

- **Handle the negative with professionalism and grace.** Let reviewers know you appreciate the feedback and will work harder to rectify the situation where possible. If your company offers an exchange policy or some kind of guarantee, let that be known. Though it can be difficult, try not to be defensive or refute what they have said.

Look at the Big Picture

Setbacks aren't setbacks at all. They are great opportunities for learning and making your marketing approach excellent. When struggling with setbacks or mistakes, go back to your reason for starting your business. Get back in touch with that purpose and feeling. Review your marketing plan with your mission and vision. It will remind you of who it is you are passionate about serving and how you can help. This may mean getting away from the office for a few hours, half a day, or more to get your head back in the game. Sometimes, the only person you need to convince is yourself.

 WARNING

- When handling negative reviews, beware of offering discounts or free replacements or services to make up for the bad experience. This can train customers to leave poor reviews in order to get coupons, products, or services for free.

Tracking and Metrics

Marketing actually works, but does yours? How do you know what worked and what didn't? Some of the business owners we have run into perform one aspect of marketing and then based their opinion of success on the number of sales they achieved. If they did not receive the sales they desired, they blamed the marketing.

Worse yet, business owners decide the success of a marketing strategy or campaign based on how they *feel* about things. I (Victoria) felt as though a monthly networking workshop I had offered for the past two years had run its course. However, when I looked at my metrics and assessed where clients were coming from, I found 25% of my new clients had attended this workshop. Even though I felt bored with the strategy, it worked well. So I decided to keep it as part of my marketing mix.

In your marketing plan, you set goals that you wanted to achieve by a certain date. Now, it is time to review these goals to see how your marketing efforts performed.

During the execution phase, there were metrics we encouraged you to collect that you will study here.

High-Achieving Marketing Process™ Step			
Meet	**Goal or Target**	**Actual**	**Difference**
• Marketing While Networking			
• Open for Business			
• Content Marketing			
Remind			
• Press Releases			
• Consultation as a Marketing Tool			
• Packaged Deals			
Cement			
• Newsletter			
• Email Marketing			
Increase			
• Social Media			
• Advertising			

Assess the Positives

If you have set a goal to reach a 20% open rate for your latest email campaign and you reached 30%, assess what went right in this campaign. Did it:

- Get the ROI?

- Reach the target audience?

- Drive in new business?

- Move a neutral audience one step closer?

- Inform or educate to cement you as the expert?

Assess the Opportunities

Something not so great is bound to happen sometimes. In fact expect something to go wrong on each marketing campaign. When that happens, this is not a time to run and hide; rather, address the issue and be vocal about the solution.

What did not work so well:

- *Missed goal.* Did you miss the number you wanted to reach? Did you fall short of your financial goal? Maybe the goal was set too high or the message did not reach the target audience. Whatever the case, missing the goal is a learning experience and an opportunity to fine-tune your approach.

- *Large Number of Unsubscribes.* If you use email marketing or newsletters, a large number of unsubscribes may mean you might have fallen into repetition or seem too pushy with your product. Make sure you assess your approach and service offering to avoid people turning off your message.

- *Bad review on social media.* See the Dealing with Marketing Setbacks for more details on handling bad reviews.

- *Remember, a complaint is a gift.* When you receive negative metrics or bad reviews, you can understand what to address so you can improve next time.

Assess Your Product or Service

Reach out to your customers to see how your product or service is working. Ask them open questions mixed with multiple-choice: "What are your opinions of the product or service?" "What would you improve?" "Would you recommend the product or service?" Then ask questions where the answers could range from "Definitely" to "Never." Keep the survey short and ask every customer in order to remain consistent.

 **NEXT STEPS**

- Assess positive and negative metrics for the purpose of modifying your marketing approach.

- Use the metrics as a baseline to set your next goals.

- Remove tactics that are not working for you.

Modify

After this step, you will have modified your marketing plan and made changes to the approaches you will use on the next marketing cycle.

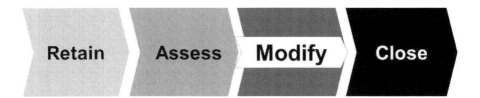

Modify Your Marketing Approach

When small business owners think about change, swinging the pendulum all the way in the other direction is the tendency. But is it wise? Sometimes small tweaks can be better than wholesale change.

Modifying your approach can be something to which you can look forward. Few companies can execute every marketing strategy all at once. After executing one marketing approach, look for opportunities to send the message out another way. It keeps the audience wanting more. *Ask Your Customers.* When you sent the last campaign and did not get the response you hoped for, take the campaign to individuals you trust to provide honest feedback and ask their opinion. *Check Your Goal.* Are you within 10% of your goal? If so, then you reached your goal. If not, study your approach. Maybe the message isn't resonating. Increase the goal if you hit your target easily. If that's the case, perhaps you did not set a stretch goal, your pricing is too low, or maybe you hit a gold mine. Whatever the case, check to see what improvements can be made.

Repackage Your Deal. Perhaps your deal was unattractive because you added a clearance item that no one purchased in the first place. Tacking on rotten onions won't help customers purchase if they didn't buy them the first go around. I (Victoria) offered a twelve-week program to help business owners create their marketing plan. It was packed with the foundational pieces and lots of advanced strategies. Though prospects had interest, they were reticent about committing to the twelve weeks and having to wait that long for a completed plan to implement. This resulted in low registration. I repackaged the program to be a six-week program to put together just the foundational plan. Not only did registrations increase 53%, I also was able to convert 10% into an ongoing program to help them implement the plan and add those advanced strategies.

Mix It Up. Marketing should never remain stale. Mix up your messages, pictures, and packaged deals to keep the customers wanting more.

Check Your Message. Is your message too long? Does it resonate with your following? Are you using eye-catching pictures? Ensure that your message is compelling and brief.

 **WARNING**

- Be careful not to make wholesale change. Consider a tweak, rather than an overhaul.

- Do not try to figure out what is wrong by yourself. Ask your customers for feedback.

- Don't rely on doing the same campaign over and over. Mix things up.

 NEXT STEPS

- Review your metrics to set your next goals.

- Change your approach but make subtle yet purposeful moves.

- Challenge yourself to be different.

Close

After this step, you will have completed one full marketing cycle and are beginning to prepare for the next wave. Marketing is iterative and should be done for the life of your business.

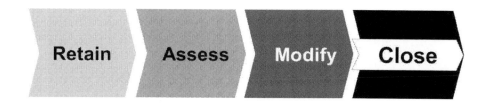

Close This Wave of Marketing

Closing your marketing is similar to closing your accounting books—If done right, you can maximize your total arsenal of strategies, systems, and tools.

The excitement isn't over. Plan for your next wave of marketing with a fresh set of eyes. What will you do next? You tracked, assessed and asked what worked. This led you to modify your approach, packaged deals, and message. But what's next? How do you look at the next wave of marketing differently?

New or Emerging Markets

Emerging markets are new people you would like to provide products and services to within the next year or so. To identify your next emerging market ask yourself, *How long have I been marketing to this market segment? Is it time for me to expand or grow to my next market?* Markets shift over time and you have to keep your products and services relevant. This is the same for marketing.

Perform market research to understand new trends in your industry. Gather this new information to see if you can update your offerings. What messages will enable you to break into this new market? Where does this new market live?

New Product or Service

Is it time to freshen up your product line? What services can you add to your offerings? If you do make a change, how will it affect your brand? What new message will you have? Is it newsworthy? Use the assessment of your marketing efforts to determine changes you can make to extend your product line. For example, garden service workers may extend their service to cleaning leaves from gutters.

Assess Your Customer

Has your market changed? We had to change our message to address those who want to work strictly in the cloud. Relevance will always keep you reviewing your message and offerings. Don't just sell your product. You will be missing out on something important, namely understanding the people who purchase from you.

Assess Your Service

Are you providing that outstanding service? Does your message match your service? By reevaluating your message, product offerings, and expanding your market, you can start the High Achieving Marketing Process over in good faith.

We close by telling you there is a wonderful plan for you and your business. Relax, be open minded, and creative. Be confident. You can do it! Stay the course, and remember that it is all right to make mistakes. It is worth the effort. You and your product or service will make a difference.

"For I know the plans I have for you," declares the LORD, "plans to prosper you and not to harm you, plans to give you hope and a future."

Jeremiah 29:11 (NIV)

Third 30 Days
Implementation Checklist

Retain

- ☐ Identify the follow-up process for the selected lead generator(s).
- ☐ Develop a loyalty program.
- ☐ Develop a referral program with incentives of value to your customer base.
- ☐ Create a strong follow-up process to update our client base on what you are doing and what's new.

Assess

- ☐ Review what worked and what did not.
- ☐ Review your metrics.
- ☐ Give your marketing strategy enough time to work.
- ☐ Respond to reviews in a timely fashion.
- ☐ Add consultation name and takeaways to website.

Modify

- ☐ Ask your customers how they like your product or service for testimonials and feedback.
- ☐ Reestablish your goal based on performance metrics.
- ☐ Repackage your deal.
- ☐ Mix up your product offerings.

Close

- ☐ Check new and emerging markets.
- ☐ See if a product or service offering expansion is right for you.
- ☐ Assess your customer to see if you can reach a new demographic.
- ☐ Assess your message alignment with service.
- ☐ Believe in and start the High-Achieving Marketing Process.
- ☐ Target your market and have them fill out a survey to learn more about them.

About the Authors

Victoria Cook, founder and managing director for The Center for Guilt-Free Success, helps women entrepreneurs grow their businesses through coaching and training. Known for her proprietary 7-step Guilt-Free RESULTS™ process, Victoria often is in demand as a speaker. She was named a "Business Brick Builder" by the International Coach Federation Chicago Chapter in 2013. Her innovative approach reflects her commitment to building the strengths of her clients as she helps them market their businesses more confidently and easily.

Ctr4GFSuccess

CenterForGuiltFreeSuccess.com

Stan Washington, a McDonald's executive turned entrepreneur is founder and president of Honor Services Office, software that helps small business grow sales, market businesses, and process invoices easily. He has helped thousands of small businesses achieve sales into the millions. His leadership of operations and technology enabled multi-billion dollar corporations to increase sales and he is ready to share their tips. Stan also is the co-author of Peaceful Selling: Easy Sales Techniques to Grow Your Small Business.

KunakaNotes
HonorServicesOffice
HSO Small Business Innovators
HonorServicesOffice.com

Victoria and Stan met while serving on a local board of the International Coach Federation, an organization with 22,000 members. After discovering they shared a similar approach and mindset to marketing, they became passionate about working together to create a tool business owners like you could use to save money and grow a business simultaneously. The result is this resource.